BURMA JACK

BURMA

by Jack Girsham

W · W · NORTON & COMPANY · INC

JACK

with Lowell Thomas

 NEW YORK ·

Contents

BURMA JACK

1

Introductory Chapter

In the beginning was the adventure, and then the adventure story, and humanity has been hooked on both since the world was young. Tales of wild animals must have ranked high on the troglodyte's list of favorites—his cave art shows he was fascinated by the creatures that roamed the plains and mountains in his time. Imagine the fellow who had tracked a mammoth through the forest, or swarmed up a tree with a saber-toothed tiger snapping at his heels, or outrun a giant bear after stumbling into the mouth of its lair. What an avid audience he must have had when the clan sat around the fire by night and the flickering play of light and shadow provided the atmosphere as he spun his yarn.

Did the audience gasp at the danger, thrill to the climax, applaud the conclusion? Did the storyteller invariably resist

9

the temptation to embroider the details by making his feat a little more heroic, his shave somewhat narrower, than it had been? If the temptation got the better of him, here again he was an authentic ancestor of ours. To go beyond the mere facts has been a human weakness at least since Gilgamesh slew the Bull of Heaven in ancient Sumeria, since Hercules brought back the hide of the Nemean lion. I've known a few Baron Munchausens of the game trail, hunters rather inclined to strain the credulity of all but the most naïve while recreating their exploits for public consumption.

This book is the story of a different breed of hunter. The teller of these tales, Jack Girsham, belongs in the ranks of those from whom you have to pry the truth—namely, that he's taken his chances with sudden death on enough occasions to satisfy a reckless daredevil, but without the daredevil mentality. Jack is a cool professional who never looked for danger until he'd planned how to handle it. That's why I persuaded him to tell his story.

It was a strange coincidence that brought Jack and me together in 1958. At that time I was on location in Assam, the northeastern province of India, filming the television series called "High Adventure." The Borsola Circle of northern Assam, up where the forest reserve pushes into the foothills of the Himalayas, is one of the prime tea-growing areas in the world. The map of the region is checkered with tea estates hacked out of the jungle: Hirajuli, Khondari, Belseri Faizabad, Dibru-Darrang, and many others. One day a tea planter drove into our camp and asked if he might borrow one of our elephants. He explained that Belseri and the neighboring estates were being terrorized by a man-eating tiger and that the professional hunter called in to handle the situation needed an elephant to hunt the tiger in the jungle.

Now, it just so happened that a tiger hunt was the very

thing we wanted for our "High Adventure" program and we had been wondering how to arrange one. The script called for a professional hunter to arrange the drive, and of course the fact that the tiger was a man-eater would make the film that much more exciting. Willard Van Dyke, the producer of the program, handed the planter several type-written pages. "Read this script. Does your professional hunter fit the part?"

The planter scanned the pages and answered, "Yes, he does." And so, without knowing anything about it, Jack Girsham became the star of our film, and the next morning we set off to Belseri with not just one but a whole herd of elephants and all our camera equipment.

There were many details to be ironed out before we could safely or successfully film a tiger hunt. We had to pick an area of the jungle where the tiger couldn't escape, and the different phases of the operation had to be well coordinated. During these discussions Jack tended to hang back and let somebody else have the floor; but when he did speak it was obvious that he was a hunter to his finger tips, that he knew his subject from the inside. We knew a lot about making films, and Jack knew a lot about tiger hunting. As you might expect, it was not easy combining the two. Jack made what concessions he could to the cameramen, but in the end we always deferred to his judgment.

He had good reason to be wary of this tiger, for the man-eater of Belseri had already killed nearly fifty people, some of them would-be hunters. Jack himself had hunted this tiger unsuccessfully on several previous occasions, spending long nights on machans and once even using himself as bait to lure the tiger out into the open. The tiger, though, was wise to the ways of men and was not to be caught by such ruses. It had been wounded once with a gun, and, as is often the case with wounded tigers, had begun to attack men be-

11

cause it could not catch swifter or stronger animals. On another occasion a worker in the tea fields had driven the man-eater off with an ax, leaving a vivid brown scar on one side of the tiger's face. Finally, after exhausting all other methods, including traps and poisons, Jack had decided to go into the jungle with an elephant to find the tiger.

Jack had scouted the area thoroughly, and from the pug marks—the track left by the tiger's feet—he could tell approximately where our quarry was hiding. When we asked him what the chances were of driving the tiger within range of the cameras, he replied, "About fifty-fifty." Only one thing seemed to worry him: the camera. He told us half-jokingly that he was more afraid of the camera than of the man-eater.

To make the film more exciting, the hunt was conducted in the manner of the rajas of ancient Assam, in the days before firearms were invented. Villagers from the area around the tea estates were rounded up and armed with bamboo spears. Jack chose a patch of jungle at the mouth of a narrow trail and strung out the nets in a semicircle. These nets were made of jute, four hundred feet long, eight feet high, with mesh six inches square. Jack directed the elephants through the underbrush while the beaters set up a din with sticks, pans, whistles, and their voices. Any tiger in our path would have to retreat along the trail that would take him into the nets.

The plan worked perfectly. Somebody shouted, "Tiger! Tiger!" There was a flash of striped fur, a pair of blazing eyes glared back toward the noise, and the beast scrambled ahead, desperate to escape. The elephants crashed through after him. The beaters redoubled their efforts. The tiger chase was on!

At the opposite end of the trail, the cameras set up behind the nets kept grinding away. The spearmen were posted where they could make their thrusts through the mesh of the heavy ropes. A cry of exultation went up as the tiger bounded from the trail into the clearing and sprang into the nets. The spears struck home. Baffled, snarling, wounded but not crippled, it pulled back as if to retreat, heard the elephants advancing up the trail, and decided that the only safety lay ahead. Again it charged the nets. Another array of spears pierced its body.

The tiger thrashed around violently, roaring, clawing, and biting at everything within reach. Then it turned away from the nets, staggered a few yards, and collapsed. The hunt was over.

It was a well-organized, well-executed tiger hunt, and it made an exciting film. The only sour note was that the tiger killed was not the man-eater of Belseri. It had no brown scar on its face, and Jack recognized its pug marks as those of a cattle-killer he had tracked several times previously. (Ironically, the real man-eater of Belseri was finally killed by a Gurkha watchman who thought it was a deer.) The hunt was a success, though, in that it gave me an opportunity to talk to Jack Girsham and get to know him.

I had never come across anyone with such an unusual collection of animal stories, or such a gift for telling them in an entertaining way. By "entertaining" I don't mean inflated, much less fictionalized. I mean Jack was genuine and articulate. When you've been around as much as I have, you learn to spot those who merely claim to have survived perilous confrontations with the more savage animals and discount half of what they say. When you meet a true jungle man, you take what he says seriously. I met an authentic jungle adventurer in Jack Girsham, and I took what he said seriously.

I feel vindicated in my opinion after reading over these stories in helping to prepare them for publication. The material is even richer than I had expected. The stories, which, as Jack says, amused me when I heard them in Assam, come across just as well in print (although I'm sorry the reader can't share my reminiscence of the soft sound of Jack's voice as his tale unfolds). If you're like those of us who made the "High Adventure" film, you'll be spellbound by the Burmese folklore of the weretigers, men who turn into tigers and vice versa. As for the stories that are simply dramatic—the crafty tigers, the king cobras . . . Well, "simply" is not the right word: drama infuses every syllable and one doesn't need an overheated imagination to feel it.

It wasn't easy to get autobiographical details out of Jack. He didn't elaborate on his Burma boyhood, for instance, or his years with the Bombay Burmah Trading Corporation. Eventually, I did persuade him to fill in this background, and it makes the book much more complete and coherent than if it were limited to a mere relating of anecdotes.

So far, I have stuck to one subject, Jack Girsham the hunter. But this is the memoir also of Jack Girsham the soldier—Captain Jack, who campaigned through Burma with our own Merrill's Marauders and came out of World War II with the rank of major in the United States Army. Here is the course of the jungle fighting as seen by a participant who presents a personalized, impressionistic account of his experiences—a scout's-eye view.

Jack Girsham has also reached back into his memory for the postwar political realities as he knew them firsthand and reproduced the difficulties of the people who were dubbed "foreigners" by the recently arrived potentates—the strident politicians of Burma and India alike. I think Kipling might have been amused by the new breed of pukka sahibs, so similar to the old in their attitudes, and so reluctant to mete out equality after their lamentations about the inequalities of colonialism.

14

Introductory Chapter

This brings me to a salient point in our history of one man's life. There is little if any animosity in it. Of course Jack speaks about the bitterness he felt during the war, and he alludes to resentments he harbored at different periods. But all this adds up to a minor confession, considering the provocations. On the whole, his story is marked by a general good humor and is well balanced in every sense, reflecting the mind of a special type of man in its economy of language, lack of histrionics, and directness.

Jack likes to use the word "chap" in British fashion. Well, this is the story of a decent chap and a true jungle man, as you will discover in Jack's own narrative.

2

Burma Boyhood

You didn't become a big-game hunter in Burma just by going out into the jungle with a heavy-caliber rifle and looking around for something to shoot. You had to have a feeling for the place and the people and the animals. You had to know how to live off the land for weeks on end, without rations except those provided by the jungle. You had to get along with the villagers in whose area you were operating. You had to be familiar with the habits of the beast you were tracking or you'd never have any success—indeed it might be the other way around if you were after a tiger or leopard, bear or water buffalo.

In short, you had to know Burma.

That's where I started with an advantage over the chaps who used to come out East from England with the idea of running the Indian Empire and doing a bit of shooting on the side. The ones who tried do-it-yourself methods usually failed to get the hide or the horns they craved. The determined ones ended up being guided by professional hunters who knew their way around.

I took quite a few beginners out myself. I knew the ropes. I knew Burma. For that's where I was born and grew up. Back before 1850 my father's father arrived in India with a battalion of artillery. He was Scottish by origin, and although I never knew him, I feel we must have had a lot in common because we both admired the army, which I might have joined too except for the other opportunities that led me to become a jungle man.

This paternal grandfather of mine served for years with his battalion and died in India. He left a wife and a number of children, including my father, who, as a young man, tried working in the forest but found it too tough for him. He caught malaria, which damaged his hearing, so he took a job in the Burmese administration and went to Pegu. I remember him as an old-fashioned individual with long sideburns and a solemn expression—a Victorian type, even though he never saw Victorian England. He never learned Burmese, despite his having a Burmese wife; since she knew English, there was no need for him to speak the language of Burma in our home.

My father worked in the Pegu courthouse, as an accountant. But his main interest was religion. He read his Bible every morning before breakfast and, after saying good night to us children, he'd read his Bible again before going to bed. We all had to attend church regularly. And every Sunday he held a Sunday-school class in our house for us and the children of the neighborhood.

Pegu was a pleasant town where we lived an unhurried life, getting about on foot or by horse and carriage. My father drove a trap, an open two-wheeler drawn by a pony, with space for two in the front seat and two in the back. Before the advent of the motorcar, the trap was the fastest

18

vehicle on the streets of Pegu, because the pony between the shafts, unhindered by any great weight behind him, could trot along at a good steady pace. When more of us had to be accommodated, or the weather turned wet, we used a gharry, a closed-in four-wheeler, which seated four comfortably. Powered by a team of horses, the gharry was driven not by the head of the family but by a retainer up on the box outside.

We usually drove to market. Pegu, the capital of Pegu District and a main depot on the railway running from Rangoon to Mandalay, was often thronged with people, and big crowds came on market day. Farmers streamed in from the tilled land around Pegu to sell their rice and sugar cane to the city people. And their wives came in search of silk, sarongs, and shawls. Curios from the West were snapped up—cameras, watches, guns, illustrated magazines. Also flashlights (or "torches," as the British call them), which were useful around the house or in the jungle, for traveling along dark trails or sitting up by night to shoot big game.

Nearly all of our Burmese friends were Karens, members of a group educated at the American Baptist Mission Schools. The father of the family next door was a Baptist pastor, and I often heard him leading them in morning and evening prayers. It was his custom, after even song, to lead his children in the hymn "All People That on Earth Do Dwell." But he was not exceptional in his piety; the Christians of Burma took their religion seriously.

Like most of his neighbors, my father was a disciplinarian. We used to tiptoe past his study, a kind of alcove off the sitting room, whenever he was there. We never went in without an invitation, request, or command. He laid down this law after seeing some of his papers scrawled with the red ink that we found on his desk, a vivid hue that splashed gloriously.

19

Still, he wasn't a stern Victorian tyrant or anything like that. He wanted us to enjoy ourselves. When he had time off from the court house, he'd take us on outings. We'd load the oxcart with food, go out into the woods, and have a picnic, returning home in the evening. It was quite an expedition the times our friends and neighbors joined the party.

I think we lived a good life in Pegu. We had a lot of fun, and at the same time we received guidance through the serious concerns of life. Needless to say, much of this guidance was from my mother.

Burmese by origin and tradition, a daughter of a prosperous businessman, she was Christian by religion and morality. She believed in the Biblical rule about sparing the rod and spoiling the child, and she never ceased to warn us about our behavior or to discipline us when we stepped out of bounds. Knowing that boys could get into bad company she'd say to her own boys: "Don't mix with So-and-So. He's a gambler. You will copy him, and waste all your money, and become dishonest, and end up in jail." We obeyed her most of the time, at least when we feared she might find out what we were up to.

My mother spoke Burmese to us, teaching us the intonation that makes all the difference in this language. My father could never master the slight distinctions of pronunciation that change meanings, but he was happy to see us growing up with a fluency in our second language.

Mother took great pride in her house. We lived in a fairly large building for Pegu. The lower walls were brick and the upper floor was made of teak, the heavy, hard, black wood of Burma. A sturdy house was a necessity in that area because the rainy season monsoon dropped torrents of water on the roof and around the foundations.

My mother had a staff of Indian servants, including an

Indian cook, but she insisted on cooking most of the meals herself. We preferred her cooking, especially the delicious curries, and half the time the Indian cook would end up taking home to his wife the roast duck or broiled chops that we by-passed in favor of mother's curry. I'm glad to say she ignored part of the Burmese cuisine: we never found boiled snake or grilled iguana on our table amid the mushrooms, the rice, and the bamboo shoots. Often the main dish was a big fish from the Irrawaddy, and we usually finished with bananas or mangoes. I have fond memories of our meals back home in Pegu.

Europeans frequently ask me about certain Burmese dishes that put them off because of a rather high aroma. Ngapi, for instance. There are various recipes for ngapi, but the basic idea is to take some fish, allow them to become somewhat overage, and then press them with salt. The result is a great delicacy, as I can testify, along with those Europeans who have the fortitude to get past the smell to the taste. The same is true of durian, a fruit Westerners tend to steer clear of after one whiff. That's a pity. If you don't turn up your nose, but have a taste, you'll find that durian is like a rich heavy cream. First impressions are so strong that most Westerners won't even eat preserves made from durian, although the preserves have nothing odoriferous about them. People remember the smell, and that ends the matter for them. My mother served both ngapi and durian, and I've missed both since I left Burma.

My Pegu was a town where people of different religions lived side by side with comparatively little friction. We had Buddhists and Mohammedans along with Christians, and although each group tended to stick together—the Buddhists going to their pagoda, the Mohammedans to their mosque, and we, of course, to our church—I never knew of anyone trying to make trouble for the members of a different faith.

A little name-calling by the children, perhaps, but that was all.

Given the Buddhist heritage of the country, Buddhist shrines naturally dominated Pegu, which was only forty miles north of Rangoon and had for centuries been a crossroads of Lower Burma. The Pegu pagoda was famous, and visitors came from as far away as Europe to view the famous Reclining Buddha of Pegu, an enormous statue of the Indian prince who became the Light of Asia. Pious followers of his doctrine could be seen every day making their devotions at the shrines erected to his memory.

The jungle lay all around Pegu, bamboo jungle with the wildlife of Lower Burma scampering through it. I particularly remember the barking deer. We boys of Pegu used to fire our slingshots at them, a practice that never put any venison on the table but did accustom us to stalking and tracking. We had better success with the fruit trees. While still a young boy, I learned how to knock a mango from the tree by severing the stem with a stone from my slingshot. Later a friend of the family taught me to use a gun, and I bagged my first deer before we left Pegu.

By then I was well along in school. I had been through a kindergarten run by three sisters who had a dozen or so youngsters under their supervision. These sisters taught me to read and write. After two years I transferred to a municipality school where most of the pupils were Burmese, and where the headmaster, English by origin but born in Burma, knew how to maneuver amid the problems of teaching boys of different racial backgrounds.

The first big change in my life came when I was nine. My father died. We packed our belongings and caught the train for Maymyo, a hill town in Upper Burma on the edge of the Shan Plateau, where one of my older brothers was headmaster of a school.

Burma Boyhood

I completed my education in Maymyo. (While the government English school was closed for the Christmas holidays, my brother used to take us into his school, partly to teach us the regular subjects and partly to keep us out of mischief.) Burmese children from the area and European children with fathers in the colonial administration mingled in the classes. I really learned about religious antagonism at the high school. When pupils of different religions got into scraps, you'd hear a little Buddhist call out, "You Christian so-and-so!" And of course we knew a few things to say back.

Only a "hill station" most of the time, Maymyo had a special importance because every summer it became the temporary capital of Burma when the Governor shifted his office north from Rangoon to escape the heat. Most of the Governor's staff came up, and we had departmental officials boarding in the middle of town and soldiers stationed in permanent barracks on the outskirts. Businessmen came too, the timber bosses and heads of trading companies, who took fashionable bungalows until the return of cooler weather permitted them to shift back to Rangoon.

So, in the summer Maymyo sprang to life, buzzing with excitement. The Governor played host at his residence, wealthy magnates gave parties and dances, the soldiers paraded to the applause of crowds of spectators. We all looked forward to the celebration of Maymyo Week, which lasted more like a month and featured an array of sporting events—polo, football, field hockey, tennis, steeplechase, horseback riding, and similar contests. The boys of the town took part in most of the events. In open tournaments I played football, tennis, and field hockey, and I was on the shooting team. We wore uniforms, carried our own rifles, and took on the Mandalay team every year. The best of us got to shoot for Upper Burma against Lower Burma.

23

Shooting became my passion. With several of the other
boys, I used to go out in search of game on weekends, using
a gun I borrowed from a sergeant of the Auxiliary Force.
The sergeant let me do this in return for part of my bag—a
marsh fowl, say, or a haunch of venison. But he knew we
were both contravening the firearms regulations, and one
day he asked me, "Why don't you join the Auxiliary Force?
That way you can get a license." Being only twelve, I answered that I was too young. He then offered to mark my
age up to fifteen. I accepted the offer, joined the Auxiliary
Force, got my license and my gun, and went shooting after
that without fear of the authorities. Actually, my first gun
was defective—a double-barrel make with one broken ham-
mer. I wouldn't turn it back for anything. I used the one
barrel in my shooting until a Sikh blacksmith took the
weapon and repaired it for me.

I did much of my shooting at that time in the Pyin-
bongyi Jheel ("jheel" means "marsh"), where I could usually
count on coming home with a few water birds.

Later I began to worry about having lied about my age
to get the license. I confessed the whole thing to the principal of the school, C. W. Ainley, who wrote to the Assistant
Commissioner of Police, and I got a valid license despite my
age. Mr. Ainley knew he could depend on me as a hunter.
He'd let me and my friends go into the jungle with our guns,
merely reminding us to be back for class.

The principal's wife also took an interest in us. Once when
we brought back a boar with huge tusks, Mrs. Ainley asked,
"Weren't you afraid of that animal?" I explained that we
didn't have time to be afraid, for once we had flushed the
boar, our only thought was to bring it down before it
escaped into the underbrush. But I added that precautions
were second nature to us because we had had good teachers
to instruct us in the ways of the jungle.

One teacher was a Burman named U Paw U, who had a house on the edge of the jungle where he frequently put us up for the night or even for days at a time. U Paw U not only had a thorough knowledge of the jungle and the habits of the dangerous beasts, but he also kept an eye on us, refusing to let us go into situations that we might not be able to handle. For instance, he wouldn't permit us to follow a wounded boar. Instead, he'd leave us behind and take up the trail with his dogs. On returning, he'd explain how he advanced cautiously as the dogs followed the scent, and, when the boar was brought to bay, how he carefully took aim at a vital spot in order to kill the beast at once. He thus avoided wounding it again, enraging it more, and giving it another chance to lead him on a chase through the jungle.

U Paw U broke us in little by little. Eventually he agreed that we too understood the tricks of the hunting trade and could be trusted to go after the biggest game without becoming careless or foolhardy.

One other sport I stuck with after growing up was boxing. I fought boxers from the regiments at Maymyo, and twice I went down to Rangoon to take on civilians. One former champion wanted me to go to England, where he would be my manager and schedule bouts with the leading British boxers. "We'll make plenty of money," he promised me. "How about it?"

I might have accepted his proposition except that my mother objected. She was a strong-minded widow lady and ran our family with a firm hand. We were a big family, as she had been married twice. I had two sisters, one brother, and two half-brothers—one who was the schoolmaster I mentioned above and one who was an engineer on steamers plying the trade routes from Rangoon to Hong Kong and other ports of the Far East. I always enjoyed it when the engineer returned home with a fund of anecdotes about life on the high seas and in strange harbors. All in all, we made a merry gathering when the members of the family converged on our home at Christmas for the annual celebration.

As for boxing, my mother disliked the sight of her sons coming home with skinned knuckles or black eyes. She put her foot down when I mentioned a fistic career in England, so I stayed in Burma. Of course I kept on boxing, and of course she knew what I was doing. But my idea of becoming a professional of the ring gradually disappeared. I found that when I became a hunter my work in the jungle ruined my skill with the gloves. My timing went off. After a long spell of shooting, I had to begin training all over again. An occasional touch of malaria forced me to rebuild my strength and stamina. You can't become Champion of Burma, not to mention Champion of the World, that way. However, I enjoyed pretty good success until I hung up the gloves for good.

Needless to say, most of the neighboring boys wanted to join the army when they grew up. We loved to watch the troops on dress parade, or at target practice, or tramping in from maneuvers. There were British soldiers and Indian soldiers and Gurkhas from Nepal—the whole martial spectacle of the men who stood guard on the Burmese outpost of Empire.

The Gurkhas were my favorites. While some regiments came and went, the Gurkha Rifles were stationed permanently at Maymyo. Along with their colorful uniforms and gleaming weapons, they had such a fine band that I used to cycle down to the encampment of the Gurkha Rifles just to hear the bagpipes. What a stirring sound when the notes floated away, slapping against the near-by hillside! The bagpipes suited these tough Nepalese warriors. The way they played the bagpipes suited me.

In spite of having government headquarters there half the

year and soldiers all year round, the people in the Maymyo area were not all what you would call law-abiding. The tradition of the dacoits remained. We were familiar with tales of these robber bands hiding out from the authorities and preying on travelers. At times the dacoits seemed to have disappeared, but out in the jungle you never could tell what you might run into. It was common enough to meet bandits and smugglers, a trigger-happy lot, always on the lookout for local policemen or government agents, always ready to commit murder rather than be brought back in irons to face a prison sentence. Many confrontations took place on lonely jungle trails in the dark of the moon. Lawmen vanished, only to be found days later riddled with bullets. Lawbreakers entered villages feet first, having been killed resisting arrest. But enough got through unscathed to make the game worth the candle. They could hide among the local people and even pass through Maymyo with no one in authority the wiser.

Once, when I was about twenty-one, I went out hunting with an experienced jungle man, an old-timer from the Shan Plateau. One night we sat up in a machan waiting for a tiger that never appeared. It began to rain in the morning, so we returned to a bamboo hut on stilts he had built in a clearing, overlooking a jungle trail between two villages. I was lying on the floor next to the fireplace while he roasted some Indian corn, when suddenly he turned his head as if he had heard something. He got up, went to the door, and looked out. Instantly he turned, gave me a sidelong glance as if to indicate that he was being watched, and said to me under his breath, "Lie still where you are. Don't move. I can't say anything more. Some men are coming."

I obeyed him. I froze where I was, face down, hugging the floor where the bamboo was split and spread out with crevices between the slats wide enough for me to see the trail underneath. There was a scuffing in the undergrowth. Some small trees parted, and a man with a rifle came along the trail. He carried two tins by a strap around the back of his neck. I knew, as anyone familiar with that part of Burma would have known, what was in the tins—opium!

A file of men, also armed with rifles and similarly carrying tins of opium followed, perhaps twenty in all. They disappeared down the trail, vanishing as quickly and silently as they had come.

The old man turned back from the door. "You can get up now," he said. "They knew me, knew I was no threat to them. But they might have taken you for a police officer. They wouldn't have asked many questions. They would have shot you without hesitating."

These smugglers might have traversed Burma along the "opium roads" leading from China or Thailand. Or they could have been transporting the opium of the Shan States, where in season you see acres of white poppies like snow on the hills. The drug was legal in Burma, but only a certain number of businessmen held licenses to handle it. As a result, a lot of under-the-counter selling went on. Enough money could be made in this way to tempt men into the life of smugglers. They transported the opium through the jungle to their contacts in Mandalay or Rangoon and pocketed sufficient cash to live it up in the cities until the time came to hit the opium trail again.

Another time I was out with a couple of chaps on the trail of a big boar. It led us down into a valley, where we lost it, and I had to scout around to pick up the track again. This time the hoof marks were much wider apart than before. The boar had broken into a run. In fact, he was running as fast as he could. Something or somebody had scared him. No use trailing him any further. He would careen on for miles, widening the distance between us at every bound.

As we started down from the topmost ridge of the neighboring valley, I caught a hint of a distinctive smell on the breeze. The scent grew stronger. "That's opium!" I exclaimed. "That's opium!" one of my companions agreed.

We went forward very cautiously into the wind that was carrying the odor of the drug toward us. After about three hundred yards of a trail snaking in and out through the hills, we saw a number of blankets hanging in a line. A man sat on our side of the blankets, his rifle across his lap pointing at us. My own rifle was across the crook of my elbow pointing at him. Either of us could have shot the other by simply pulling the trigger. It was a tense moment, but I had the sense to keep walking with a show of unconcern. Once past, I never looked back. I knew he was trying to make up his mind whether I was connected with the police. Any suspicious actions, and he would have cut the three of us down. I could feel the sweat trickling down my back by the time we were out of range.

The rest of the gang, of course, were behind the blankets smoking opium. When smugglers took a break, they generally lay down with their pipes, leaving one of their number as a sentry. We had stumbled across just such a party. The air was heavy with what I can only call a nauseating aroma. The sentry knew I knew what was going on. He figured I'd consider the spectacle none of my business unless I was officially committed to making it my business. He was right. One rule of survival in the Burmese jungle was to keep fellows like this from going on a shooting spree. You didn't have to like opium smugglers, but you didn't want to antagonize them either—unless you were foolhardy or else backed by an American-style posse.

In line with this, I never inquired among the villagers to see how they felt about smuggling. It had been a way of life in Burma for so long that few could have taken a high moral attitude. The smuggler seemed a romantic figure, a Robin Hood of the jungle who fooled the police in a game of wits. Opium? "Why not?" they would shrug. "Haven't we Burmans smoked opium from the beginning of time?"

In my part of the country, the best place to sell opium was Mandalay, the emporium west of the Shan Plateau and the center of transportation by road, by rail, and by water down the Irrawaddy. Mandalay had been the capital of Burma in the days of the monarchy, and Kipling gave the city a romantic reputation when he wrote his famous poem. I must say I never liked the place. It lay spread out along the river, so low in relation to the jungle all around that it held the air in a stifling pocket most of the time. European officials assigned to Mandalay wanted to escape as soon as possible. Most of the people who lived there permanently were Burmans. Most of the dwellings were Burmese *bashas*, flimsy structures built of bamboo, fine for jungle living but hardly the thing for a family home. Artists and historians admired the more than two thousand pagodas, temples, and palaces of Mandalay. Not being an artist or a historian, I had a different opinion.

Every Saturday I used to bicycle to Mandalay from Maymyo, a freewheeling forty-two miles of zipping down hills and around curves. The roads weren't bad. Taxis used to cover the distance in an hour and a half. I could get to Maymyo with plenty of energy left for a football game, the weekend sport that I hardly ever missed. After the game— that was something else. Whatever energy I had left pretty well disappeared as I pedaled my way back up the hills to Maymyo. I found the road from Maymyo to Mandalay easier to negotiate when I began driving a car.

Either mode of travel could lead you into some interesting experiences with the big cats of Burma. I've lost count of the tigers and leopards that crossed the road in front of my bicycle. I learned to skid to a stop in a hurry whenever one of them appeared. A collision could have been fatal for me.

As for driving, here's an example. I once drove some people from Maymyo to Mandalay to catch the train to Rangoon. At the twenty-first mile, which we called the halfway house, there was a cement tank with water for car engines that were getting overheated. It was a moonlit night, and as I eased into a flattened area on the left to park and take on some water, I noticed a big blackish blob on the rim of the water tank. The blob grew larger in the glare of my headlights, and finally I realized that a large tiger was lying with half his body in the tank, lapping up water. As we kept coming, he scrambled to his feet, leaped down from the tank, and ran into the bushes.

Even Rangoon was not safe from adventurous cats. I knew Rangoon quite well as a boy because my mother often took me down there for the holidays. She loved the city. For one thing, her clan was congregated in Rangoon, relatives who kept her gallivanting from one house to another to hear the latest about births, deaths, weddings, and other events of great importance to her. Secondly, she loved the hustle and bustle of the capital. "Come along," she'd say to me, "and we'll go to the bazaar." At the bazaar she'd have the time of her life window-shopping at the stalls, haggling over prices, buying whatever she wanted or could afford.

I never liked Rangoon any better than Mandalay. I was not interested in being petted by relatives. The bazaar was not picturesque to me, only overcrowded. The whole city had too many people and not enough trees. The only time it appealed to me was when the Water Festival produced a carnival spirit for three days of the hot season. Then we spent our time eating at booths along the street and throwing water at one another from buckets, ladles, and bags. It was all good fun, but that was the best I could say of Rangoon. Later I boxed there for championships and once became something of a local hero by beating up a tough Filipino who had knocked a row of Burmese and British army and navy boxers galley-west. Even then, I left as quickly as I could. The jungle was always calling me. And it was near enough for me to answer the call.

A few years before World War I a tiger wandered into Rangoon and actually climbed up onto the Shwe Dagon, the wonderful golden pagoda of the capital, one of the most beautiful and sacred examples of Buddhist architecture. The tiger perched on one of the balconies, causing intense discussion about what he was doing and what should be done about him. The British officials would have had him shot out of hand, except that the Burmans protested: "This tiger has come to worship. You cannot shoot him. It would be sacrilegious." They considered the cat a wandering spirit, probably some person who had come back to earth as a tiger and wanted to pray at the shrine of Buddha. This kind of thing seems perfectly reasonable to Buddhists, who believe in the transmigration of souls. The Burmans hoped the animal would leave of its own accord. However, it stayed put. Since it could not be captured on the balcony, the authorities finally decided it was too dangerous to ignore any longer and had the tiger shot.

That couldn't happen today. Nor could many of the other things that we took for granted. When I think back to old Burma, I'm struck by how much it's changed since the days when I was a boy. At that time, it was still a province of India, and it remained a province, using Indian currency, until the separation of 1927. With so close a connection, and many resident Indians, we in Burma inevitably felt the effects of Mahatma Gandhi's independence movement. Along with a large Indian population, there was a smaller Chinese population, and native Burmans disliked both foreign groups because they tended to take a superior attitude, were good at business, and collected a major share of the money. The Indians came in for much criticism because they were so numerous.

Europeans didn't necessarily feel any antagonism toward these incomers. In our house we had Indian rather than Burmese servants. My parents, my father especially, being so religious, disliked the Burmese habit of using foul language and employed Indians, who, for some reason, did not share the habit. Most of the Indians who passed through our house came from the Bengal area and were Hindus; a number had made a longer trek from Madras in South India and were spirit worshipers. The distinguishing difference was that the Madrasis had no compunction about eating the sacred cow, while the Bengalis flinched at the very thought. Anyway, between them they taught me to speak their Indian languages, which stood me in good stead years later when I became a hunter in Indian Assam.

My Burma was a good place to be. We may not have had too many conveniences of modern life, but we didn't miss them. Shelter was easy to find or build. Food was easy to gather. Berries, plants, fruit, and edible roots grew everywhere in the jungle. A lot of rice boiled with a little meat made a fine stew. And every stream had its fish, which swam inland during the floods of the rainy season and were left trapped in pools when the water receded. We could bail out a pool, take the fish, dry, cut, and salt it, and have a nice aromatic dish of ngapi.

I knew all about Burmese life by the time I left school

33

to look for a job. I liked it. The thought of leaving Burma never occurred to me. Since Maymyo didn't offer many opportunities, I went south to Rangoon to see what might turn up.

3

Cutting Timber in the Teak Forest

The first job that turned up was a post in the Customs Department of the government. It really wasn't my cup of tea, but I took it in order to stay solvent until I could find something more in my line.

As the gateway to Burma, Rangoon needed a big staff to keep the books on a tremendous volume of imports and exports. Freighters from the great seaports of the world would sail in from the Bay of Bengal, through the Gulf of Martaban, ascend the Rangoon River, and tie up at the piers along the waterfront. They brought quantities of manufactured goods —clothing, paper, tools, bicycles, and cars. Moving the other way were native Burmese products like rubber, rice, cotton, and teak.

I had no passionate interest in shipment inspections and

bills of lading, but I mastered the technicalities during the few months I worked in the office. Actually, I would have left sooner except for the football team. Each department had its team, and there was a hot rivalry between them. When I arrived in Rangoon, I made the Customs Department team, which ran up a record against opponents from Rangoon and the hinterland. My superiors wanted me to keep on playing.

That was the only bright spot. I didn't like a desk job; I didn't like Rangoon; and I was happy to shift over to the Bombay Burmah Trading Corporation, which took me out of the office and sent me back to the jungle.

The Bombay Burmah Trading Corporation, the largest timber firm in the Far East, had a network of subdivisions from India to the border of China and into Siam. Its prosperity lay in the exploitation of the teak forests. In fact, that was a major reason why the British were in Upper Burma. When they had been confined to Lower Burma, the company gained timber rights from King Thibaw, who ruled in Mandalay. I'm not clear about the details, but a disputed contract was blamed for the Third Burmese War of 1885. Thibaw's high court ruled that the company had removed many more teak logs than it paid for. The Burmese judges demanded that the directors pay an assessed 73,333 pounds (the pound sterling was the world's hardest currency) into the royal treasury. You can judge the wealth of the Bombay Burmah Trading Corporation in 1885.

The British in Rangoon were angered by the ruling. They feared French penetration of Upper Burma from Indo-China. After much maneuvering aboveboard and under the counter, a British army moved north toward Mandalay, and the Third Burmese War ended in a speedy victory for the soldiers of Queen Victoria. Thibaw and his wife, Supayalat,

Cutting Timber in the Teak Forest

went into exile in India. A British administration took over in Mandalay.

The change occurred in 1885, less than a decade before I was born, so I grew up in the backwash of the events that transformed Burma. I heard all about the misdeeds of King Thibaw, who had been completely dominated by the ruthless Queen Supayalat, instigator of the mass murder that made Burma's last royal reign a byword for sadistic atrocities. In Mandalay I often walked over the corner of the courtyard where Supayalat had had her executioners club to death dozens of members of the royal family, potential rivals she wanted out of the way. The extermination took place during two horrible nights while within the palace music blared, dancing girls performed, and Thibaw drank himself into a stupor. At this corner, the victims were buried and then elephants stamped the loose earth flat over their graves.

Supayalat, the Tiger Woman of Burma, ended up placidly enough. She outlived Thibaw (who died in 1916), and then received permission to return to Burma—but only to Rangoon, not to Mandalay, where she had ruled as the King's consort. The Burmans didn't hold her past against her, as far as I could tell; some had even liked her. Besides, it was all ancient history, wasn't it? There might have been a popular movement to restore her to the throne. That's why the British put Mandalay out of bounds to her. I never saw Supayalat, but I remember when she died in 1925.

My Burma was, therefore, the Burma of the British Raj, a jewel in the imperial crown of Queen Victoria's successors. As a youth, I never saw any real opposition to British rule until 1920. Before then, the Burmese people were satisfied, and the independence movement only slowly gathered headway, triumphing as late as the period after World War II.

37

The Burmans accepted European benefits: good administration, better policing of the countryside (formerly the preserve of the robber bands, the dacoits), hospitals, machinery. No one tried to deprive them of their religion, their language, or their dress. They adopted business practices to share the new wealth developing under capitalism. They joined the governmental departments. They even took up football and boxing, Western style.

The typical Burman saw no point in becoming violent, not when the rule of strangers from Europe at least had the virtue of being competent. The educated class changed first —they were impressed by the victory of Japan over Russia in 1905. Then came the real turning point, the rapid development of Mahatma Gandhi's campaign against colonialism in India.

When I joined the Bombay Burmah Trading Corporation the system of extracting timber was good and worked smoothly most of the time. However, animosities did occasionally cause hard feelings between the bosses and their workers, as some Englishmen took a very highhanded attitude toward the Burmans, having come out East with the whiteman's burden mentality and the belief that they were a cut above the "natives." Some Burmans couldn't take this treatment, but others shrugged it off—for a time.

The company was a power in Burma. Its experts charted the entire country for the teak forests that formed the staple of the timber business. The flags on their maps followed the contours of the terrain, tracing the pattern of forests from the western hills on the Indian border, through central Burma where the Irrawaddy Valley forms the nation's axis, to the Shan Plateau extending east to what was then French Indo-China.

It took quite an organization to keep the business going. Simply finding the right trees to fell was a science in itself.

Cutting Timber in the Teak Forest

Teak forests don't occur in masses of huge trees growing close together and providing many logs in a small space; the trees grow about a dozen to an acre. And trees had to be four and a half feet in girth at breast height from the ground, for the Forest Department would not permit girdling anything smaller. And getting at the giants was a problem, because teak forests are not pure teak. Between and around the trees clumps of bamboo grow, forming a kind of shield which has to be cut through. Fortunately, usable teak trees are easily identifiable: they may grow to a height of a hundred fifty feet, and to a circumference of twenty-five feet; their leaves are huge, perhaps twelve or fourteen inches across.

The value of teak timber derives from its being immensely strong and heavy yet easily worked at the mill into attractive boards. We of the company had impressed on us the good money to be made from bringing Burmese teak to market, especially to the British furniture and shipbuilding market. The company spent money to make money. It had thousands of jobs of all kinds for people both skilled and unskilled.

At the bottom were the fellers, the laborers who toppled the trees and cut the logs and did the more menial tasks. We got them through contractors who scouted the villages of the interior with wage offers that were enormous by local standards. Then there were buffalo contractors who gathered about a hundred animals at a time for the task of dragging logs to rivers and streams. They received good rates according to the number, length, girth, and weight of the logs, and the distance from the piling area to running water. Most important were the elephants working at both ends of the operation. They picked the logs up at the site of the felling and dragged them to the level area where the buffalo could take over. They waited by the river to work the logs in the water after the buffalo had dropped them.

The elephants took out thousands upon thousands of logs that would otherwise have remained untouched. Even after years of experience, I still marveled at the ability of an elephant to bring a heavy log out of hilly, rocky terrain. An elephant can do better than a man or a machine in moving straight through a bamboo clump: a machine needs roads and a platform, the elephant will find both for himself.

Willingness to do the job, understanding of the animal corps, knowledge of the timber and the terrain, timing according to the season, above all cooperation at each phase—these were the factors that had to be put together. They *were* put together. They made the Bombay Burmah Trading Corporation successful.

I went up the Irrawaddy as an assistant to an official who ran a work gang in an area bordering the Chindwin River. Joining the camp, I met the hired hands and began to learn the logging techniques. Suddenly my immediate superior became ill. He went back to district headquarters for medical attention and never returned. The company promoted me to the position of the man in charge, which was more responsibility than I had bargained for. I breathed easier when I found it wasn't too difficult to direct timber work because some of my men had been with the company for thirty or forty years. They were professionals who rarely needed to be told what to do. They knew their assignments, whether they were sawing timber, two men at opposite ends of a long saw, or caring for sick elephants, or anything else.

I was their boss, and I had a boss above me to report to, and he had a boss above him, and so on until you reached the people at the top in Bombay and Rangoon. The biggest bosses were British. They handed out the regulations for the entire Forest Department of Burma. The district heads were also British. Each Conservator of Forests had divisional forest officers under him, who had to show that they were making good when he came through on an inspection tour. These inspectors were not the most popular people in Burma. They were the ones who, more than any others, took a superior attitude toward the Burmans who worked for them, and the Burmans resented it, especially those who knew they were fitted for better jobs that were always carefully preserved for the British. For myself, I took the prejudice of the obnoxious type in stride—at the start anyway. The first man I reported to was named Hager, a very nice chap who was pleasant with me and my workmen, and so I was willing to overlook the attitude of the inspectors who bothered us only once in a while. His successor, a fellow named Gilman, rubbed me the wrong way, but I never let it get me down. I was too happy to be away from a desk, and in the jungle, and, of course, on my own much of the time. Later, a series of unbearable pukka sahibs got on my nerves, and I chucked the job with the Bombay Burmah Trading Corporation; but the first six or seven years suited me.

Each year I would submit a plan, showing how many elephants and mahouts I would need to bring out so many thousand logs, giving one set of figures for the rainy season, another for the cold season, and adding them together to indicate what I expected to produce during the next twelve months. During those years I shifted from district to district, searching for the best trees in each place, deciding the best ways to get them down and out. The object was to cut the timber and bring it to the nearest stream. Apart from terrain and distance, you had to know how high the stream would rise when the rains came, or you might end up with a magnificent pile of logs, all neatly stacked where they'd be left high and dry.

In each area a block of timber was marked on the map, a compartment so many miles square, and I'd be granted a certain amount of time to clear the compartment. At the end, I'd report to the authorities that no more trees worth felling were standing there—and that was when an inspector came around to check. His main concern was whether any marketable timber had been missed. That didn't mean simply that the big trees had to be down, for the inspector went over the stumps, taking measurements to see that no tree had been sawed too high up, leaving marketable timber untouched. There were strict tables specifying length, girth, and volume—the minimum girth, for instance, was four feet six inches—and if you cut an inch above the prescribed level, leaving that much marketable timber on the stump, you were fined.

Every so often I'd have to go deeper into the forest and see what was there. I'd take a map and have a look at the ridges and streams, trying to determine the easiest routes from ridge to ridge, from spur to spur, toward what streams, and toward the stretches of the streams where logs would be floatable. I'd figure out the spots where the elephants would drop the logs, leaving the buffalo to drag them the rest of the way. Generally, this meant taking the logs down to the level terrain, which allowed the buffalo to work with less exertion and freed some of the elephants for work in the streams.

The Forest Department started operations by girdling the selected trees in the forest. We girdled the bark right around, about three inches in, stopping the flow of sap and causing the trees to die where they stood. The idea was to leave girdled trees standing for three years because green teak is too heavy to float and gets waterlogged. The dry tree floats. So teak cutting worked by stages: some men would be girdling new trees while others were felling the trees that had been girdled three years before.

Cutting Burmese teak is not like felling timber in Canada

Cutting Timber in the Teak Forest

or the American Northwest. No one would shout "Timber!" to warn anyone else out of the way of a toppling tree. We were too far apart for that. You'd see two men working a saw on one spur, and half a mile away there'd be another pair, and so on. Just little groups out there in the back of beyond. Usually it would take a couple of men four or five hours to fell a teak tree. When they were done, they'd move on, leaving the log to the elephant assigned to it. A vast silence hovered over the area. There wasn't much noise at any stage of the proceedings, just the rattling of harness and the occasional shout of a mahout guiding his elephant.

When I read Kipling's "Mandalay," I knew he had caught the atmosphere that the Burmese teak cutters lived in:

Elephints a-pilin' teak
In the sludgy, squdgy creek,
Where the silence 'ung that 'eavy you was 'arf afraid to speak!

Cutting teak kept me on the move. I worked the Chindwin area part of the time, and then I crossed the Irrawaddy to the Shweli area. The Shweli River was a great place for a timber man. Beyond its banks grew splendid teak trees, big beautiful titans of the Burmese forest that made fine logs.

I'd report to headquarters for three days of the month, but otherwise I was on the go from one camp to the other, a few days here and a few days there. In winter I'd stay in tents. In the rainy season I'd move into *bashas*. The difference was that a tent was of little use in the rain. The interior would get soaking wet and soggy, with ankle-deep mud. So we put up *bashas* with three low walls on one side and the fourth side open. You had a floor under your feet and a roof over your head—a bamboo hut that would keep both the rain and the mud out. The *basha* remained dry during the most torrential downpour. What a relief to duck into it!

I often heard strange noises while lying in a *basha* in the jungle. Occasionally a tiger or leopard would come padding around. Whenever I heard a water pail tumbling end over end, I knew a bear had come into the compound, slapped the pail over, and been frightened into a hasty retreat by the clatter. But the sound that invariably brought me wide awake was a booming from the direction of the stream, a reverberating noise that echoed for miles around. The noise told me that the logs were shifting. The rain had caused the stream to rise, lifting the logs and driving them together, making them bang one another with terrific force.

The danger then was of a log jam. The men would be up no matter what the hour, and out no matter what the weather, collecting their elephants, riding them down to the stream, and ordering them into the water to break up those jams so that the logs could float freely. The elephants did most of the work that is done by men with poles in American logging. We'd put the logs in floating order, the smaller ones in front, and the heavier ones behind, and when the water rose high enough, the tributary streams would carry the groups down to the main river, where other men would be waiting to tie them together into rafts behind a floating boom. When the rafts were finished, the boom would be opened, and the rafts began their journey downstream to the sawmills.

There might be twenty-five hundred logs in a flotilla of twenty-five rafts for a single voyage. The rafts were big enough for men to live on, and the raftsman was one of the skilled workers in the business. The job tended to become a family tradition. A boy learned from his father how to guide their floating home downriver without piling up on a Chindwin or Shweli mudbank or overshooting a landing place along the Irrawaddy. He in turn would teach his son the trade. I've sailed with professional raftsmen who lived in raft-*bashas*, bamboo structures anchored to the logs lashed

44

together and protected overhead by canvas roofs. We lived in quite high style as we floated down the Irrawaddy River to Rangoon.

Not all the rafts went that far. Some dropped off at Mandalay or smaller river ports along the way. It was all a question of what was needed at a particular place—so many rafts, so many logs. But the biggest timber mills were in Rangoon, so that was where most of the timber went.

Being with the field organization of the Bombay Burmah Trading Corporation was unforgettable. I worked hard, but I enjoyed the work, even when a log jam woke me in the middle of the night after a hard day in the field, even when some crisis or other forced me to deal with sick men or recalcitrant elephants.

4

Elephants
and Mahouts

The Bombay Burmah Trading Corporation had an elephant camp headquarters at Mansi, on a tributary of the Uyu River, which is a tributary of the Chindwin in western Burma. Mansi was a sleepy jungle town. In my time, it had a small police outpost, a sergeant with five or six men, just to show that the government way off in Rangoon knew there was such a place. These policemen didn't have much to do. They chatted with the villagers, flirted with the girls, snoozed in their headquarters, went hunting off duty (which seemed to be most of the time), and drew a handful of rupees a month for staying there.

Most of the activity in Mansi came from the company. We kept men and animals to gather teak and place the logs in streams to float down to Maingkhaing, where they were collected and formed into rafts. One of my duties was to call at Modé during my swings through the district to see that everything was in order.

The first time I visited the area I found a small camp of little *bashas* where the mahouts lived with their families. I walked through with my Burmese assistant. At the last *basha* I saw a huge elephant standing under a tall tree. The animal was not moving its feet but moving its great body backward and forward in a rhythmic cadence. I asked my assistant, a native of Maingkhaing, "Is there something wrong with that elephant?"

"Oh," he replied, "that elephant is minding the baby. He's pushing a cradle."

I thought the man must be pulling my leg. But he kept a straight face, so I went up to the tree for a look. Sure enough, a cradle with a baby in it was hanging from a branch, and this gigantic elephant with massive tusks was gently moving the cradle from side to side. He used just enough strength to keep it swaying. He never jarred it. He would take the swing against his head, pull back slightly, and then propel it forward in a smooth motion. The baby in the cradle was sound asleep.

The sight astonished me so much that I decided to ask the baby's mother about it. We found her down at the stream washing clothes. "It is safe to leave your baby in the cradle with that big elephant?" I asked. "Won't he squash it?" The woman laughed. "Completely safe," she said. "The elephant loves babies. He's rocked almost all of those in the village. He's been doing it long enough to know how. He once rocked me in my cradle."

This was the most unusual case of a working elephant I ever came across; but the Burmans use elephants in many remarkable ways. There isn't a more helpful domestic animal anywhere as far as I know, surprising as it seems. Here you have a great hulking brute—a large bull may stand ten feet and weigh in the neighborhood of three tons—his short neck doesn't permit him to turn his head to the rear, his eyesight is poor, his brain is small in proportion to his body, he needs hundreds of pounds of fodder every day plus fifty gallons of water. That sounds as if the elephant would be about as useless as the rhino until—you look at the other side of the coin.

The elephant has virtues no rhino ever had. He is friendly toward men, docile, patient, obedient. And intelligent. He learns quickly despite his comparatively small brain. It doesn't require a human teacher to train an elephant to be smart. Nature trains him herself. Wild elephants have an amazing sagacity.

When I was a game ranger I set out to kill a couple of inveterate raiders, big tuskers that wouldn't leave the villages alone. But they outmaneuvered me. There was a herd near by, and the tuskers would move into the middle of a group of females as soon as they sensed I was around. They all understood the danger. Probably hunters had killed a few elephants in the herd, and the rest learned what to do when another hunter arrived. I tracked the tuskers for several days without getting a chance to take a shot. They would retreat as soon as they got the scent, and the females would charge forward in my direction, trumpeting angrily. The whole herd had figured out two things: they knew I was after the two bulls and they knew I wouldn't shoot any females. The best I could do was keep them all moving away from the cultivated area and back into the jungle.

The story doesn't end there. Another hunter was scouting this elephant herd. I saw his tracks, the pug marks of a big tiger. He had his eye on a tiny calf that—judging from the footprints, which were smaller than a saucer—had been born a week or ten days before. Tigers dote on baby elephant, and this tiger stalked the herd hoping to cut off the youngster and kill it.

The mother of the calf understood better than I the danger lurking in the undergrowth. She never let the baby fall behind as the herd moved on but kept the little fellow up ahead of her, slightly to one side, within easy reach of her trunk, taking it slow while the others went on ahead. Once the young one got a little too far away and suddenly gave a squeal of terror. Instantly there was a tremendous crashing through the undergrowth, and loud screaming, and dust flying around. The big elephant came smashing forward at top speed, with trunk up and ears cocked. She jolted to a stop, and a moment later I saw the calf standing between her forelegs as she stared into the jungle. Her behavior could mean only one thing: the tiger was there.

I always hated to see a tiger pull down a young elephant. When this mother moved on toward the herd, guarding her calf step by step, I said to my Burmese tracker, "Let's go to where the herd is grazing right now. This elephant will come along, and the tiger is sure to be right behind her. He wants to make a meal of that baby. I want to get him before he does."

We circled around and climbed a tree over the trail between the herd up ahead and the mother lingering behind. She came along shortly afterward, guarding the calf, stopping every few steps to glare into the jungle and trumpet furiously. The Burman nudged me. "Look," he whispered, "that's what making her angry!" He pointed into the undergrowth. The tiger was crouched behind some bushes, staring hungrily at the calf.

I reached for my gun, but the elephant moved on at that point, and so did the tiger, disappearing from view, obviously stalking the pair and waiting for the baby to get so far away that he could grab it before the mother came up. This time the pair got into the herd. The baby was safe for the night.

The next day the same thing happened. The herd moved to a new area. The mother kept hanging back, measuring her pace to that of her calf as he struggled along. The tiger kept prowling around the calf. My tracker and I kept after the tuskers.

We were off to one side in the jungle when the entire herd began to converge, stamping and screaming. There was no mistaking that sound. They were getting the scent of the tiger as he circled them. We quickly climbed a tree so that we could see what was happening in that patch of the jungle. The elephants were facing in one direction. The tiger was slipping through the bushes in an attempt to get downwind from them. His hunting preoccupied him so much that he forgot to watch out for hunters who might be after him. He dodged the wind, but he didn't dodge my bullet. That was one kill I felt happy about, because I love baby elephants. I would like to have patted this one's mother on the head. Between us, we had saved him from the tiger.

A wild elephant knows all kinds of tricks. Going up a steep hill, he will curl his trunk around trees or bushes and lever himself up. Going down, he will stretch his legs out before and behind and slide down on his belly. For all his bulk, he will stand motionless, not even twitching an ear, when he senses danger. Heedless of the noise he makes when out in the jungle, he can also raid a cultivated banana grove by night so silently that he will not alert the owner who may be sleeping only a few yards away.

This last is one type of elephant that has to be shot. A few elephants can ruin the economy of villagers who have nothing to make a living from except their banana groves, rice paddies, and other crops. It's terrible for a farmer to come out in the morning and find that a herd has played merry hell with his livelihood. When this happened, or seemed about to happen, we game rangers were called in to shoot enough elephants to give the rest the idea that they would be better off deep in the jungle.

For an animal lover like myself, it was gratifying to see how often elephants learned from experience. Realizing after a couple had been shot that the survivors would suffer the same fate if they kept raiding the crops, they'd quite often move off of their own accord.

I came across one astonishing example of elephant sagacity, or instinct—or I-don't-know-what. During one season I shot eight or nine elephants more or less in a line along a range of hills bordering some rice paddies. The next season the tracks of the herd showed that they had come back to the paddy fields at the same place. When they reached the spot where I had killed the first elephant the year before, they seemed to sense something. They paused, milled around, and then retreated into the jungle. Some time later they returned. Now they reached the spot where I had killed the third or fourth elephant, and again they felt that something was wrong, and again they swung around and retreated. They made a third approach to the same paddy fields, emerging near where I had killed the last elephant. This time they were so disturbed that they not only retreated but abandoned the area. They weren't seen by the villagers for another two years.

Of course, there is the elephant who won't be frightened off. Typically, this is the rogue, the "man-eating tiger" of the species, the one that goes for human beings and has to be shot as a danger to life even more than to property.

Different causes will make an elephant go mad. An old bull may be driven from a herd by younger rivals. That leaves him in a constant rage, and he will charge at anything in his path, man or beast. A young elephant may attack man because man has attacked him. It's the same as with the man-eating tiger. Somebody goes out with an inadequate gun, or doesn't shoot accurately, and merely wounds the elephant. The beast roars off into the jungle, nursing a wound that refuses to heal. Maybe the bullet has caromed off a tusk into the soft flesh at the base of the trunk where a very sensitive nerve runs up into the head. The elephant suffers from a continual throbbing pain. He remembers that a human being did this to him. He becomes savage, out for revenge. And he'll charge any man, woman, or child who gets close to him.

The rogue likes to ambush his victim. He'll stand stock-still in the tall grass, wait for a human to approach, and then light out after him. This is about as terrifying an experience as anyone can ever have.An elephant, traveling at twenty-five miles per hour, is much faster than a man and can easily run him down in an open field. Obstacles mean nothing to an elephant. Where a man has to go around a big thorn bush or a clump of bamboo, the elephant will plow straight through. I've seen a bamboo clump leveled with the roots torn up, which takes enormous weight and power. A man wouldn't have been able to push between the trees, but the elephant simply pushed them over because he couldn't be bothered going around.

Someone with no jungle experience might think he could evade an elephant by letting the animal pound toward him and then jumping to one side. What he fails to grasp is the hugeness of the beast. Even if he escaped the trunk and the tusks and the head, he'd almost certainly be grazed by the belly, which widens out on either side. And being grazed is all it takes to smash a man to death.

A rogue, being gifted with an elephant's intelligence, may go on killing people for years before he's cornered and shot. I went after one in Assam that had killed more than sixty victims: he had been wounded by a hunter. Having learned his lesson about the peril of a man with a rifle, he'd never come out of the jungle until he had surveyed the landscape, and then he'd smash up whole villages and terrorize his section of Assam.

The huts of India were not built on stilts like Burmese huts but were level with the ground. This rogue would move in from the jungle by night, advance silently to a hut, push in the wall with his head, and trample over everything and everyone inside. In one instance a twelve-year-old boy, sound asleep on his pallet, was crushed to death by the elephant's foot. Another time a woman with two small children woke up in time. She cried out, but was too frightened to run when she saw the monster shambling toward her hut. All three were crushed to death in the ruins. Other villagers were gored or trampled. Many who got away alive saw their homes devastated.

This creature had the biggest footprints I've ever seen. I'd spot them here and there, recognizing them every time as he dodged me and kept me guessing where he'd turn up next—perhaps *he* recognized *my* footprints. It was rather chilling to imagine him screened by a clump of bamboo, watching me enter a village, rifle in hand, and then hustling off while I was still inspecting the damage he had done. But that's the way of the experienced rogue. He fooled me at one place after another. I like to think that I would have caught up with him in time, but in fact he reached the end of his career of crime by accident. He was in a part of the jungle where he thought he was safe, when a hunter who wasn't even looking for him stumbled on him and brought him down.

The first rule in elephant hunting is this: Don't take the chance of creating a maddened beast that will turn into a rogue. Use a sufficiently heavy gun to kill the animal, and place your shots scientifically from within a range near enough to be effective. You should kill your quarry with one shot if possible. This can be accomplished in five ways, as I frequently explained to the amateurs I took elephant hunting. If you shoot an elephant behind the shoulder toward the chest cavity, you can place your bullet in his heart. If he's standing still, he'll drop in his tracks. If he's running, he'll fall and careen to a stop.

Most opportunities, however, involve hitting an elephant in the head, and here there are four basic shots depending on the angle of approach. Let's take the most frightening experience—when the animal spots you and comes charging head on, ears acock, trunk up, screaming with rage, making the earth shake with the force of his attack. What you do is wait until he's twenty-five yards or so from you; draw an imaginary line from one eye to the other, bisect the line, and aim two inches above the bisection; press the trigger. Your bullet will knock him stone dead.

When the elephant isn't facing you directly, you have three possibilities. If his head is canted at a three-quarters angle, pick out his eyebrow and plant your bullet just above it. If he's at right angles to, you choose the ear as your target —making sure that the other ear is in direct line of fire, because if his head is not straight the bullet may be deflected by the bony obstruction of the ear. Finally, if you are approaching the elephant from the rear, remember that every elephant has a habit of flapping his ears and select a moment when the ear is flapped forward, noting the mastoid behind the ear and firing at the depression over the mastoid.

All of these head shots have a single goal: to cause the bullet to penetrate the brain through its center. If your line is off, you may knock the beast down only to see him get up again. With a bullet in the brain, he may be badly wounded but not anywhere near dead. You may be the first to die if he catches up with you.

One word of advice. Be sure your nerves are in good shape before you face a charging elephant, or you might get your kill and still come out a nervous wreck. I once hit one with a perfect frontal head shot. He went down, but his momentum sent him careening toward me. When he stopped, the tip of his trunk was only about ten feet from me. He was too close for me to run or fire again. Dead or alive, had he reached me, I would have ended up under a few tons of elephant. My knees were shaking as he drove into the dirt. Sweat poured down my back. It took me at least an hour to recover. I've known men who had similar experiences and never did recover, never went out loaded for elephant again.

In shooting elephants, the impact of the bullet counts more than the velocity. The same applies to tiger shooting. A tiger has been known to cover a hundred yards after being shot through the heart. With his speed and weight, he'll bowl a man over and maul him even when mortally wounded.

Both tiger and elephant hunters should carry rifles with sufficient striking power to knock the animal down. The biggest caliber I ever used was the .600, with a bullet as thick as a man's thumb. The smaller dimensions were effective too—the .500, for instance, and the .425. Any of these will give an elephant a shock that will jar him to one side or send him crashing to earth, and even if he staggers to his feet, he'll be too stunned to go right after you. However, I'm not advocating simple adoption of the biggest gun you can find on the market. I decided to discard the bigger bores because the recoil was so powerful that they'd virtually knock me down while they were knocking an elephant down. For example, the .600, a small cannon that shoots a flash of yellow flame along with the bullet, gave me a shoulder so bruised

and swollen I could hardly raise my arm. After a little ex-
perimenting, I went to the calibers that took care of big
game without taking care of me at the same time. With a
.425 I could be sure of firing as many shots as necessary
without being laid up for repairs each time.

I've been talking about wild elephants and how intelligent
they are. As for tame elephants, what man has done is to
teach them a new vocabulary. In the jungle they speak in
natural sounds—cries of alarm, screams of rage, and the
low grunting noise that indicates pleasure. The tame elephant picks up a human vocabulary of twenty-five or thirty
words which he understands perfectly. I don't know how
many he could learn if somebody took the trouble to test his
intelligence and memory. The Burmese stopped the lessons
when the pupil had mastered a limited set of useful terms.
Such as:

Yoo! (Pull!)
Oung! (Push!)
Met! (Kneel!)
Tah! (Stand!)

This type of vocabulary was fundamental in the timber
business. It enabled the mahout to tell his animal what to
do and when to do it.

Most of our mahouts came from jungle villages. They
were uneducated men who weren't interested in any other
sort of job, rough-and-tumble characters who liked rugged
outdoor work, especially when it concerned elephants, which
they knew a good deal about since they had lived in elephant
territory since they were children.

The city people of Burma did not consider the job of the
mahout a romantic one. They thought only *loo mike,* a man
of bad character, went into this kind of work, that he wasn't

fit for anything better, and that any villager of sense and ambition would necessarily choose a better way to make a living. I never believed any of this. I handled mahouts for several years and found them very friendly fellows, not the kind you'd have trouble with, except on rare occasions. They were good, reliable workers and took pride in themselves and their elephants. The company hardly ever had to fire a mahout for laziness, incompetence, or insubordination. These men liked what they were doing and were paid well. They had no reason to be troublemakers.

It's a beautiful thing to see a mahout working with his elephant. They become good friends, often friends for life if the mahout gets the elephant when they are both young. You may find a man of forty and an animal of forty who have been together for thirty years. But it doesn't take that long to form a team. A few months of close association are usually enough to convince both that the elephant will instantly obey the mahout's commands, and that the mahout will see to all the elephant's needs.

Their comradeship reveals itself in many ways. Take bath time, for instance: an elephant lying on his side in a stream while his mahout clambers over his huge flanks, giving him a good scrubbing with a kind of foamy soap made from a special Burmese root. When the scrubbing is finished, the mahout will polish the elephant's tusks until they gleam in the sunlight. All the while, the gigantic beast will have a pleased look on his face, like a cat having its ears scratched.

We had elephants of all ages, from newborn calves to fifty-year-old tuskers. The half-grown animals were put to work as pack animals, carrying us and equipment from place to place. The older ones did the heavy work of moving the teak. They'd be on the job for nine months of the year, resting from April to June, the hot, dry season in Burma. It's dangerous to work them in the heat because they have dif-

ficulty breathing and don't perspire freely enough to main-
tain body temperature at the right level—we'd have had
Rangoon in a dither about the cost of replacements.

During the season of cooler weather we kept the elephants
on the job four days a week and gave them the other three
off. They were turned loose each night, forefeet fettered so
they could only shuffle along, and allowed to forage for
themselves in the jungle, thus permitting them some freedom
to roam and cutting down our food bill. Each morning each
mahout would go looking for his charge, who, in addition to
being hobbled, so he couldn't wander too far, wore a bell
made of wooden clappers to make finding him easy. A
mahout could unerringly pinpoint his own elephant from
the sound of the clappers, no matter how many others might
be in the same part of the woods at the same time. If all was
quiet, the mahout would look for footprints, which were a
certain method of identification to him. He might find that
the quiet was deliberate. Elephantine intelligence includes
a skill in rendering clappers virtually noiseless by filling in
the hollow parts with mud.

The morning routine was for each mahout to track down
his elephant, summon it to him, take hold of one of its ears,
order it to "lift," step onto the curved trunk, and "ride" up
to his seat on its neck. The pair would then travel together
back to camp, where the mahout would saddle his mount,
and attach a harness with heavy chains extending backward
on each side. At the site of the teak felling, the chains would
be fastened to a log weighing perhaps a couple of tons. The
elephant would lean into his harness, taking the force of the
load against his chest. After a moment of straining, the log
would begin to move. On level terrain, the problem would
be simply to keep it moving to the pile. On rough terrain,
the elephant might have to maneuver the log over rocks
with his feet and tusks, or send it bouncing down a cliff by

butting it over the edge. At the pile, he would boost his contribution into place, sometimes rising on his hind legs to push it to the top.

These were the log piles—in shallow streams, or on mud flats, or along banks where high water could reach them—that rose with the rain and gave off the telltale booming sounds, providing the elephant corps with the additional task of going into the water to break up the log jams that might be forming. At the same time, the rafts had to be constructed.

And this is where the intelligence of the elephant really seems fantastic, far beyond that of a cat or a dog or a horse. A mahout will keep up a constant chatter directed at his companion on the job, and the creature will somehow pick out the right commands to obey. I once watched a mahout on the bank giving instructions to his elephant in the water with a string of oaths and other compliments so complex that I had trouble following them myself. "Not that log," the mahout called out, "the one on the other side! I told you quite plainly to go over to the east, not the west! Don't you know the east from the west? Haven't you got any sense? Do I have to go in the water and show you how to move logs? So, you got that one into place, did you? All right, now go over to the side upstream! Upstream, you numbskull! Can't you get it right the first time? You'd better get this raft together or you'll catch it! I'm not going to wait all day! Speed it up!"

The mahout kept firing this kind of talk at the elephant, who understood what the mahout was shouting about by the tone of his voice. Patiently he pushed one log into place and then another, moving around in the water from point to point, assembling them in the necessary pattern for the trip downstream. This went on all afternoon, with the elephant changing direction to handle different logs as the order came from the bank. The final command was to wade ashore: "Come on! You can stop working for now! After all your mistakes, it's a wonder we ever got the raft together!"

The elephant came up onto the bank, lifted the mahout onto his neck, and lumbered off toward the camp. The understanding between them was marvelous.

Off duty, a mahout will play with his elephant. He'll proudly show the tricks the animal can do. "Let's go!" the mahout will say. "Let's see how you can hop on one leg. Right leg first. That's good. The people are impressed with you. Now show them something else. How about a hand-stand?" The elephant obeys, raising his huge bulk up onto one hind leg, then onto the other, then going up on his front legs for a real balancing act. Of course, commands to sit, lie down, and roll over are simple for him to understand and obey.

They're very gentle, these biggest of land animals. The dangerous elephant is the exception. Naturally, accidents do happen, and once in a while a mahout gets stepped on. Normally a mother elephant will allow you to play with her calf with as little concern as a cat with kittens. Just don't frighten the youngster, because if he raises a cry of fright, his mother may go for you; so it pays to keep a safe distance from her. Even then, however, the incident passes quickly, the mother quieting down as soon as the baby does.

The one tame elephant that often becomes savagely violent is the male afflicted with musth, which is usually connected with a state of sexual excitement. The beast may be already turning savage when glands near the eyes secrete a fluid that drips down on either side of the face and especially when it gets into the mouth, which sends him into a paroxysm of madness. That's when he may gore other elephants, and turn on his mahout. Many mahouts have been killed by musth elephants. Logging camps have been thrown

61

into a turmoil. Yet, there is usually no need to kill the villain of the piece because he will come through this phase and regain his former composure. A week after killing his old master, he may be back at work under a new mahout.

Sick elephants also required special handling in our logging camps. An elephantine bellyache had to be treated with medicine on the same scale, and the Burmans, with their timeless comprehension of the beast, would concoct brews strong enough to kill a man. They'd boil vines, leaves, and other ingredients, fill a tub, and pour gallon upon gallon of the stuff down the throat of the patient. Nine times out of ten, the cure worked.

Folk wisdom came to my aid one time when I saw an elephant with a badly swollen hind leg. "Cobra bite," his mahout informed me. "Are you positive?" I asked doubtfully. "Here, I'll prove it," he said, and, whipping out his knife, he deftly lanced the swelling with a twist of his wrist, plunged his hand into the opening, and proceeded to pull out gobs of slimy, greenish, poisonous-looking matter. "Only a cobra can do that to an elephant," he observed. All the mahouts looking on nodded their agreement. I never questioned from then on that cobras do bite elephants. A full-grown elephant won't die, but he'll suffer from a bad limp and fever until the venom works itself out of his system.

Lancing is rarely as simple as in the above case. If the elephant sees the knife, he will usually shy away from it, backing up or turning in a circle to face you, because he knows the instrument you're holding is going to hurt him. We had an elephant in one camp with a monumental eruption along the shoulder that pained him so badly he could scarcely stand it. Yet he refused to let anyone approach that shoulder. After some fruitless maneuvering, a plan occurred to me. "Give me the knife," I said to the mahout. "You keep him occupied in the front while I slip around the rear. When I reach the other side, I'll signal you. Then you pull his ears forward and hold them. That way he won't see me with the knife." It worked. The ears acted like blinkers on a horse. He never noticed me advancing along his flank. I reached the sore shoulder, plunged the knife into the swelling, and gave a rip. The elephant winced and then halted. A moment later he began to "purr" as the infected matter poured out of the broken skin, relieving the soreness. If you're ever had a boil lanced, you know how he felt.

Minor cuts, bruises, and sprains we pretty much left to the elephants themselves. If working might aggravate the condition, we'd take the invalid off duty until nature brought him back to health. With pregnant elephants we also let nature take its course, and, after the event, we might present the lady with an extra bunch of bananas as a reward for presenting us with a baby to add to our herd. Incidentally, whether he knows an elephant's period of gestation is a good test of a jungle man. If he knows it's eighteen months for a female calf, and twenty-two for a male, he's a pro.

When you talk to a Westerner about elephants in Burma, the first thing he thinks of is a man in a swaying howdah holding a rifle at the ready while beaters comb the forest for big game to drive into his path. That wasn't the kind of hunting I did, although I rode an elephant on some occasions. It's safest to be on one whatever the circumstances. Elephants are usually not afraid even of tigers; on the contrary, tigers are afraid of them. Occasionally a tiger will attack, gashing an elephant with his fangs and claws, perhaps pulling the rider off into the undergrowth. But that's exceptional. As a rule, you're safe as long as you're on an elephant.

Once in a while I'd take a company elephant for a hunt, although not for tiger. I learned how to handle the animals from watching the mahouts, who taught me to ride. I'd say to a friend, "Hey, get off for a spell and let me have a go." I mastered the art of sitting on an elephant's neck with my feet pushed up behind his ears, and guiding him to the left or right, making him turn around or stand still by movements of my feet and body.

When I went hunting, I'd find a fettered off-duty elephant, take his fetters off, and say, *"Met!" Met!"* As soon as he obeyed by kneeling down, I'd sling the fetters across the back of his neck, climb up, give him the command to rise, and drive him into the jungle. It was great fun to push fearlessly into the elephant grass—twelve feet high, almost level with my eyes—which a man on foot has to avoid for fear of encountering a big cat or a short-tempered buffalo hiding there. Stalking lesser game in an open field, I could get close to deer and pigs—which won't run from an elephant—while I was too high for them to catch the human scent. Shooting them was like shooting sitting ducks. I returned to camp with many a stag, boar, and game bird for the pot.

I hunted and worked with mature elephants and made pets of the young ones. Baby elephants are wonderful creatures—playful, inquisitive, and trusting with human beings. Soon after birth, they develop immense strength, and by six months an elephant can hold you on his head without dipping his neck in the slightest. If you try pulling his trunk, he'll give an affectionate jerk and send you tumbling head over heels. I knew a young elephant who enjoyed having me swing between his tusks; he could flip me up in the air with a mere toss of his head.

During my early period with the Bombay Burmah Trading

Elephants and Mahouts

Corporation I had a five-year-old female calf who became as
fond of me as I was of her. I used to put a basket on her
saddle with a few small objects in it, and she'd follow along
behind the big elephants feeling quite satisfied that she was
doing her share of the work. We called her Ma Pu, which
means "Miss Short," because she had a stumpy figure lower
to the ground than most.

Ma Pu liked me so much she'd force her attentions on me
at the most awkward times. Once when I was working on
my report about what I'd found on an inspection tour Miss
Short came up to the table and began to push her head
against it. "Take her away!" I called out. "Take her away!"
Someone drove her off with a cane, the young lady screaming and trumpeting in protest. She circled around, came up
to me from the opposite direction, picked up a glass with her
trunk, and dashed it to the floor, smashing it to pieces. I
had to order a mahout to chain her to a tree—where she
could make all the noise she wanted without preventing me
from getting on with my job.

During one period I went off to another district, and
didn't see Ma Pu for two years. When I returned I saw her
mother, and I knew a seven-year-old calf is not separated
from the mother. I walked out toward the elephant herd,
calling, "Ma Pu, *la, la, la*"—which means, "Ma Pu, come,
come, come." The response was the clank-clank of the clappers of an elephant bell and a shuffling sound coming
toward me. Here was the young elephant I had known, now
wearing a bell, fettered like an adult to prevent her from
straying. Recognizing me, she started exploring my pockets
with the tip of her trunk. She remembered that I used to
carry a delicacy she loved—tamarind, a kind of bean rolled
up into a ball with a little salt, which functions as a mild
sort of laxative or tonic. In the old days she knew she could

count on me to produce a ball of tamarind from my pocket, and this time she thought she was a big enough girl to find it for herself.

I don't know whether it's true that an elephant never forgets. I do know that one baby elephant remembered her favorite sweet for two years.

5

Tiger Trails

I bagged my first tiger when I was sixteen. The hunt took place at Zibingyi, two stations along the railway from Maymyo, and while there wasn't anything spectacular about it, I remember the occasion as my earliest success with the big cats.

I was out in the jungle when I came to a village where the people were badly frightened. The head man said to me, "A tiger is in the area! An ox has been taken! You're a hunter, and we want you to sit up over the kill."

Pleased by their confidence in my hunting prowess and excited at the prospect of shooting a tiger, I agreed. In no time (the Burmans are really marvelous with their knives) they'd cut some bamboos and fastened them across in the center of a bamboo clump to form a stable platform just large enough to sit on—approximately three feet by two feet. I climbed up on the machan and sat where I could get a bead on any big cat that came into the vicinity of the dead ox. One of the villagers asked, "As soon as we hear a shot, shall we come back here to see if you've hit the tiger?" "No, don't take the risk," I answered. "I'm not an expert, I'll be on the tree, and it will be dark." The head man replied, "Then we'll wait until morning before we return." And he led the others back to their village.

Since it was summer, the ground around the bamboo clump was rather bare to begin with—the vegetation parched by too much sun and too little rain—and building the machan had flattened the grass even more. There was a young moon, so I had a good view of the kill in the patch of jungle where the tiger had left it. And there I sat. About eight o'clock the tiger came. He entered the patch, stood near the remains of the ox, and looked up the trail where he knew human beings had passed. Satisfying himself that he was alone, he walked around the area at a distance of twenty to twenty-five feet from the machan.

Finally he gave me a favorable angle, and I fired a charge of buckshot behind the shoulder, driving forward into the chest cavity. He gave a grating snort, leaped into the air, came down on four wobbly legs, and staggered into the undergrowth out of sight. He began to roar a moment later, tremendous roars so loud that the ground seemed to shake. That frightened me. I didn't know how badly he was hurt or what he was still capable of doing.

Between roars, he made a gasping sound, a labored panting that I'd never heard before, which didn't make me feel any more secure. I guessed that an hour had passed since I hit him, when his voice started to weaken. The roaring tailed off into coughs and gasps. Silence fell. That didn't dispel my fear—now I couldn't even tell where he was.

The night grew cold. The mosquitos came in swarms, harassing me for hour after hour. I had to remain there and take it. To have climbed down in the darkness with an injured tiger only a few feet away in the undergrowth would have been sheer madness.

Finally dawn came, and a couple of villagers crept close enough to ask what to do. I told them to come on in, skirting the spot where the tiger had disappeared. They climbed up and joined me on the machan. We held a council of war.

"The tiger was here and I shot him," I said.

One of the villagers remarked, "He must be dead, or else he's gone away."

The other fellow countered, "How could he have gone away if he was in the same place roaring for nearly an hour?"

We agreed to climb down. Cautiously we looked around. Sure enough, there lay the striped gold-and-black body of a tiger. The two villagers threw clods of earth and clumps of grass at him as I held my gun at the ready. He was dead.

It seems somehow anticlimatic as now related, but it was a beginning.

After that first tiger, I kept shooting the big cats over the years and decades until my list ran to forty-seven. Not a record number, but I wanted a good reason why a given tiger ought to be shot—*before* shooting.

There was often a feeling of regret in this business. I'd get to know tigers by their footprints, and seeing a particular row of pug marks in the jungle was like meeting an old friend. There was a time when I used to go down into the bushes in one district to cut bamboo, and I'd come across the footprints of a striped cattle-killer that had been terrorizing the villages. We even saw one another on occasion, but invariably he was too far out of range for me to chance a shot that might only wound him and turn him from a cattle-lifter into a man-eater. I developed a friendly feeling for this fellow—he was like a familiar part of the landscape. Well, eventually I did shoot him. And then I felt remorse because we'd never meet again. I was so used to identifying him by his footprints that a picture of him would rise in my mind whenever I saw them. When those marks vanished, and I knew I'd never see them again, I was really very sad. The jungle he had stalked never seemed quite the same afterward.

Whatever success I had with tigers and other beasts of Burma came from a genuine respect for them (except snakes, for which I had no respect at all). I took them on their own merits and got to know the habits of whatever species I was after—where they lived, what they ate, how they reacted to man, and so on. I got to the point where I could think as they did, where I understood why an animal would take one riverbank instead of the other, or why he would return to an area months after abandoning it for a district perhaps twenty miles away. I learned much about hunting from watching the greatest hunter of them all, the tiger.

The tiger is the fiercest and the wariest animal you can meet. A human being who gets within ten yards of a deer feels puffed up about his performance. He thinks to himself, What a wonderful stalker I am! He forgets that all he has to do is shoot the deer, while the tiger has to creep close enough to catch the quarry and kill it.

A tiger on the prowl is a beautiful sight. You'll notice him padding down a game trail, looking entirely unconcerned, when suddenly he'll stop dead in his tracks and listen. You can tell where the sound is because his ear is cocked in that direction. He doesn't turn his head; he knows his prey might be alerted by the slightest movement. He simply cocks that one ear. If he doesn't hear anything more, he'll continue on his way. He may climb a tree to look over the long grass—yes, tigers do climb trees, not with the agility of the leopard who lives in them, but with enough skill to reach a vantage point on a big limb. The wise jungle man will learn to climb as well as the tiger, and for the same reason.

Another trick the tiger uses is to wait at the end of a trail for his quarry to come out. The hunter can do the same when it's too dangerous to keep moving ahead. Suppose you hear a tiger fighting a boar in a clearing where a well-used trails leads off into the jungle. Find the end of the trail, choose a concealed place which affords you a good shooting angle, wait there patiently, and one beast or the other may appear. Should the boar make a run for it, or the tiger decide he's taken on too much to handle and retreat, you may well bag the beast that comes along to the place where you're stationed.

I mention this type of battle in the jungle because, although I never watched a fight between a tiger and a boar, I heard one and I saw the results. A terrific racket erupted one morning while I was out stalking in some scrub jungle, a mass of thorn trees that you can't move through very easily. When you get a thorn hooked on to your shirt, you start to pull yourself free only to have your elbow or your shoulder caught. You end up in one place disentangling yourself. Your progress is slow.

The noise told me that a tiger and a boar were going at one another, and I knew I might get killed if one of them came rushing toward me while I was caught in the thorns. So I stopped and waited to see what would happen, meanwhile shifting my gun into position for a quick shot. The din didn't let up for what seemed like hours to me. There was savage snarling, high-pitched squealing, and a violent thrashing around in the grass. Then silence fell, and I thought they might have moved out until I heard some groaning, grunting, and gasping. I said to myself, They're getting ready for the next round! But the battle didn't start again. All remained quiet. Naturally, I didn't advance in that direction. I decided to return to the village, moving back down the trail with a vigilant eye for every movement in the grass, and wait for the morning to see what had happened.

At daybreak I went back to look for footprints emerging from the grass where the battle had raged. There weren't any. Well, you don't just walk into tall grass when you know an injured tiger or wild boar might be in there. I told the boys of the village to bring a herd of buffalo to the place, and to drive them through the grass.

We were letting the buffalo break trail for us when we heard a loud snarl. The buffalo came dashing out in all directions, wild with fear. I told the villagers, "One animal is in there, anyway! He must be hurt or he would have run away when he heard us coming! We can't leave him. First let's get the buffalo back here."

It took us a long time to round up this herd of frightened buffalo, but eventually we got them moving again. The first of our animals to reach the scene began to shake themselves and roar, and soon the herd was stamping around as if greatly disturbed by something they saw. We started to push them, and they scattered.

Soon I could see what was wrong. A big tiger was lying motionless in the grass. He was ripped and gashed in the face, throat, and chest. But the boar had killed him by driving a tusk into his belly. When we skinned the tiger, we found that the liver was damaged, the tusk having penetrated that far.

Looking around, I noticed a trail of blood leading off into the grass at one side of the clearing. We followed the trail and found the body of a huge boar. The tiger had hamstrung him, and had clawed and bitten him in a frightful manner. The boar's scalp was practically torn off, part of it overlapping one side of his face. He must have had a terrible time after pulling himself away from the tiger and rolled about in agony, over grass, bushes, and saplings, for quite a considerable time before he died of his injuries.

The tiger and the boar had killed one another. They were well matched for the ferocious battle, the life-and-death struggle I had heard but not seen. The tiger measured nine feet two inches in length, and weighed about four hundred pounds. The boar looked about two hundred fifty pounds, a hefty brute in excellent condition. His tusks were wicked weapons, eight inches along the curve, pointed, sharp, like a couple of daggers. He had the thick, heavy, leathery hide of the species, like armor plating compared to the comparatively thin skin of the tiger. This boar would have made a good match for any tiger.

It wasn't hard to figure out how the battle must have developed. The tiger kept attacking continuously, and he might have finished the boar off except for that rip in the liver. Even then, it wouldn't have been easy. The tiger had to adopt a deliberate strategy—attacking, backing off, maneuvering, feinting, and attacking again. The boar, on the defensive, kept slashing back at his tormentor, occasionally bounding forward to deliver a thrust. The boar must have been groggy when the tiger managed to hamstring him. These pigs generally keep their heads down when they're wounded, and they find it hard to breathe, hard to get their wind back. The tiger probably got through his defenses from the side, seizing him by the hind legs, cutting the hamstrings.

The boar couldn't maneuver very much with one hind leg out of commission. All he could do was stand his ground and try to meet the tiger head on. He was being worn down, and had suffered fatal injuries, when he gave the toss of his head that impaled the tiger on one tusk. The two mortally

73

stricken antagonists then crawled off to die where we found them.

Jungle cats are unbelievably strong. One incident I like to cite to make the point has a twist to it. I was on my way home from a small hunt—mostly deer and feathered game— when some villagers met me in great excitement. They said that a buffalo had been taken, and that the killer must have been a tiger because only a tiger would be strong enough to carry such a big animal away. They wanted me to sit over the kill and shoot the tiger. I wasn't anxious to do it, since evening was coming on and I felt tired from two or three days in the jungle. However, I allowed myself to be per-suaded by the argument that more domesticated animals might be taken. I said I'd sit watching until eight o'clock, and if the tiger didn't show up by then, I'd climb down and go home.

We followed the drag through the grass and scrub and into a part of the jungle with tallish trees. We found the remains of the buffalo, an enormous creature, about half a mile from where the kill had been made. I climbed a tree, settled myself in a fork and waited. There was no time to make a machan. Anyway, I expected to be only a couple of hours at the most, so I wasn't too concerned about the discomfort of a tree fork, or about the drizzle that began to fall. You hardly feel the rain when you're straining your eyes for a glimpse of a tiger you suspect may arrive at any moment.

The grass was all trampled and flattened down, giving me a clear view of the area, with the hindquarters of the buffalo toward me, and its head pointing the other way. Only part had been eaten. There was more than enough left for another good feed, and a tiger usually comes back for a second helping when he's made a kill that size. My gun was loaded with buckshot and ball in different chambers. I was ready. I waited.

Presently, toward dusk, the birds behind me began to scold. They set up a cacophony of squeaking and chattering—agitated sounds meaning that an enemy of some kind was approaching. Glancing over my shoulder, I saw a huge leopard padding along the trail. All spots, no stripes!

The leopard moved up to the buffalo, lay down along it lengthwise, and began to tear chunks of flesh from the shoulder. I fired with ball, hit him where the spinal column joins the skull, and ended the affair. The villagers began to converge on the sound of the shot. I called out, "It's all right! Come on in!" They were as surprised as I was when they found the animal wasn't a tiger. The leopard had dragged the buffalo for half a mile, which just shows how strong leopards are. And of course tigers, being half again the size, are that much stronger.

Tigers are cunning. I'll always remember a man-eater I tracked over a whole district, a troublesome cat who hadn't been living on human beings for very long, but seemed to have mastered all the tricks of evading hunters. Every time I went out in one direction where he'd been reported, he seemed to sense something and would be gone. He had his beats, moving from place to place, and he'd killed six or eight people when I took up the pursuit.

I was tramping from one village to another with an old man, a Burman who worked for the Bombay Burmah Trading Corporation. He didn't know English, but he knew Burmese, and, more important just then, he knew the ways of the animals. He was a typical jungle-wise Burman, and I often relied on such people after I became a hunter. They had been studying the beasts all around them. They understood the species, and they understood individuals too, the fact that a tiger or leopard will develop its own habits—using particular trails coming and going, remaining here for so many days before shifting to another area, running from the approach of a human being or circling back to have a look, and so on.

This old Burman listened to what the villagers had to say of the tiger that terrified them. He inspected the pug marks, noted the various places where the brute had appeared, and finally said he was sure we'd pick up the trail if we went in one direction, and that we could work around and intercept the tiger. We went off together in that direction. Sure enough, we came upon the tiger.

This one was a female, a tigress. We spotted her at the edge of a village, slinking through the grass, stalking an old woman washing clothes in the stream about a hundred yards away. Anyone unaware of the tigress would have considered everything normal and peaceful. On the opposite side of the stream some boys were firing stones from their slingshots at birds in the trees. A group of men were cutting bamboo with their long knives. And here was this old woman hard at work on her washing, completely oblivious to the tigress slipping hungrily toward her.

Fortunately, we arrived in time to stalk the tigress. She might have come out of the grass close enough for me to take a quick shot, but the men in the distance caused her to veer away. We went right after her. She started up the bank toward a point where she could sneak through the grass and leap upon her prey directly below. That was when I fired. My first bullet knocked her down. As she turned over and struggled to regain her footing, I dashed over and shot her again. That was the end.

The opposite of the man-eater who hunts human beings is the tiger who won't seize an opportunity to commit murder or mayhem on the most helpless. Any Burmese hunter could mention dozens of cases. Here is an example that I saw at first hand.

It happened on the Myitnge River, which runs east of Maymyo and turns south into the Irrawaddy below Mandalay. For a dozen miles the river is flanked by high cliffs, and beyond them the terrain is so rugged that no villages had been established there. Fishermen were familiar with the Myitnge because fish swam in schools in the deep pools along the banks, and frequently a man would return home with a fifty-pounder, or more, for his wife to drop into the family pot.

We had fishing camps on the banks overlooking the best pools, and we'd often stay overnight. One time a seventy-year-old man from the Shan Plateau accompanied us, a taciturn old fellow who preferred to keep to himself. At night he'd leave us, move a hundred yards or so along the bank, and go to sleep in the sand. When the sun came up, he'd join us for breakfast and some more fishing.

One morning I went out before sunrise in search of a sambar I had heard belling on the hillside—making the strange metallic sound that resembles a bell. I went as far as another fishing camp without seeing him, and, since dawn was about to break, I retraced my steps. When I was about six hundred yards from my camp, I suddenly noticed unmistakable pug marks in the sand: a tiger had traveled the same route, and his tracks were fresh. He had come down the hill, paused at the stream, and turned in the direction of the camp. I followed his footprints until I saw a human figure lying in the sand—the old Shan man, sound asleep. The tiger had been there minutes before, surveying the figure for himself. The marks of his forepaws indented the sand about four feet away from the sleeper. Then the track continued on past to one side, reached hard ground, and disappeared.

77

I shook the old man awake. Before he could get up, I said, "Here, look at the visitor you had while you were sleeping." I pointed to the pug marks. The man turned on his elbow, inspected the tiger's tracks, and remarked coolly, "He came up to have a close look, didn't he?"

The man remained nonchalant, despite what I considered a close shave, because he recognized the animal's footprints. At breakfast he told us, "I knew this tiger was in this area. And if you're interested, he will be back again, going down the way he came up this morning. He is usually away for fifteen days at the most, unless he runs into hunting or some other disturbance, in which case he will go up into the mountains away from the river to wait. When he feels safe again, he will return to the river and continue downstream. If you go upstream from the camp right now, you will see his footprints again. If we hadn't been here, his tracks would have continued straight along the river." A couple of boys took the old man at his word. They went upstream, returned a little later, and said they had found the pug marks exactly where he said they would be.

This kind of jungle wisdom came from experience. The man had been coming into the area for over fifty years. In one season he would fish, in another he would scout the surrounding hills for the famous Burmese orchid. And so he became familiar with the wildlife of the Myitnge area. He learned the behavior patterns of deer, bison, buffalo, leopards, and tigers, and he felt undisturbed by his visitor of the previous night because he knew that this tiger, far from being a man-eater, left men alone as long as they left him alone. That was true of all the Myitnge tigers.

"After all," the seer from the Shan Plateau observed, "man-eaters go where human beings live. There's no reason for them to be out in these hills. To survive here, a tiger has to be able to catch deer, and there are plenty of deer for him to stalk. Otherwise, I wouldn't be sleeping by myself every night, believe me!"

Every jungle man is asked which of the two big cats is the more dangerous to go after when it's wounded and hiding in the tall grass. I'd say it's the leopard. He's almost as capable of mauling a man to death as the tiger, and yet he's smaller. He can hide under a clump of grass that wouldn't conceal a tiger; so you may be close to stepping on him before he charges. But there isn't much difference where hunting them is concerned. They're both ferocious when wounded, crafty to the verge of the supernatural, and protected in the jungle by their coloration. I'd always take the same precautions going after a leopard as going after a tiger.

6

Hunting Humor

Do animals have a sense of humor?

They certainly communicate their feelings in complex ways. Monkeys chattering peacefully in a group will suddenly scatter when one of them gives a particular kind of cry, for they understand he's telling them to make for the higher branches because a leopard perhaps, or a python, is approaching with a simian entree in mind for the next meal. A barking deer will alert all of his kind within earshot about a pack of wild dogs on the prowl—a harsh bark like a dog's, entirely unlike the provocative call he gives during the mating season. Species can communicate. The screeching of a treeful of birds informs other birds, monkeys, deer, even buffalo and elephants, that a tiger has arrived, while ordinary bird song doesn't disturb a single creature.

A successful hunter learns to interpret a whole system of animal sounds. They frequently guide him to his quarry.

Does this system include laughter? Do animals have a

81

sense of humor? I don't know. But if they do, they must tell one another some hilarious stories about that strange creature called man. They've got plenty of material for high comedy. Hunting is full of humor.

I knew a British officer who fancied himself a hunter. He had read books written by Jim Corbett and others who had gone after big game in India, and he knew all about tying a bait, and sitting on a machan, and shooting the tiger or leopard attracted by the bait. He had a platform built overlooking an open patch of jungle, had a goat tied at a good shooting angle, and went out after dinner to bag a cat.

A leopard came, sprang upon the goat, and began to maul it. There was a tremendous mix-up in the clearing. The leopard snarled ferociously, the goat screamed in terror, and the hunter raised his gun for a shot. The report caused the two animals to break apart, like boxers obeying the referee. A moment later only one remained. The leopard had vanished. The goat lay stiff. The hunter had killed it with his shot. He bagged his bait and scared off the cat.

Another time this same officer asked me whether there was good shooting in a particular area. I told him he could find plenty of game at a small stream with a salt lick frequented by hundreds of animals. This was near our buffalo camp, a site chosen by the buffalo contractors so that their herds could wallow in the water and the mud. The wild animals would come down by night, after the daily bustle subsided. "Douse the lights in your *basha*," I advised the officer, "tell all the men in your vicinity to keep silent, and you'll be able to get a deer."

He took my advice. Quiet reigned over the camp the night he chose to go hunting. Around midnight a shot rang out from near the salt lick. His men assumed that he had spotted a deer and opened up with his rifle. Then came another shot, and another, and another. . . . He fired a dozen or so times within a few minutes. They couldn't figure out why he took so many shots in the darkness. "Maybe", said one, "a herd of elephants have come up to his *basha* and he's trying to drive them off."

The men went down to the salt lick to find out. They found the officer very pleased with himself. "Sambars all over the place," he explained. "Big stags with magnificent horns. I brought down a number of them." The men wanted to go and have a look. "Don't be silly," he said airily, "I know what I'm doing. When you've hit big game, you don't go after them on foot in the dark. The stags I shot got up and staggered off. In the morning we'll find the blood trail and follow them. They can't have gone very far."

He and his men were out bright and early next morning. They found the blood trail in the grass, followed it, and came to the corpse of . . . a buffalo belonging to the camp contractor. They went on and discovered another timber camp buffalo. Then another. And another. The hunter had decimated our buffalo herd, killing seven of the beasts that the day before had been dragging teak logs to the stream. He had mistaken them for sambars and had kept banging away until none were left. He had to pay a good share of his salary to placate the irate buffalo contractor.

I once heard about a misadventure with a tiger that had a strange ending—not funny, unless sardonic humor is something to laugh at. A hunter sat up one night and bagged his tiger, which leaped into the air when the bullet struck, twisted around clawing at the air, and collapsed. The hunter put a second bullet into him just to be sure he wouldn't get up. The next morning, when some villagers arrived, the man pointed to the body stretched out near the bait. Climbing down from his machan, he strode up to it. The tiger lay completely still, its eyes closed, no sign of breathing at its muzzle or its flanks. "Dead before it hit the ground," the hunter commented to the villagers.

Triumphantly he gave the body a heavy kick in the rump. The "corpse" whirled upright, swiped at him with its paw, and crushed his skull like an eggshell. This man hadn't learned the lessons of the jungle, one of which is to beware of a big cat lying with its eyes closed. If the eyes are open in a fixed stare, the beast is dead. If the eyes are closed, it may or may not be dead. To mistake a dead tiger for a live one is funny. To do the reverse is always dangerous and can be deadly.

On the lighter side, with a happier ending, I had a good friend, a Burmese hunter from a jungle village. He never could afford a gun, but he borrowed a twelve-gauge shotgun and went deer hunting at night. He was expecting a sambar when a tiger came along toward his machan, and the opportunity seemed too good to ignore. He took a shot at the tiger. The buckshot struck the beast in the head and body, but it escaped into the grass.

Of course my friend waited until the morning, and finding no sign of the tiger, he went back to the village to ask for reinforcements in trailing it. Most Burmans are ready for this kind of sport. Besides, they don't want an injured tiger lurking near their village, so it wasn't hard to round up a dozen or so for the chase. He took the lead carrying the gun, and they picked up the blood trail and followed it into a patch of jungle dominated by a thick clump of bamboo surrounding a tall tree.

Suddenly the tiger bounded out of the clump with a roar. By reflex, everyone swarmed up the bamboo to get out of the way—everyone except the fellow who had done the shooting. The tiger came after him, and he didn't have time to raise the gun. He lit out around the bamboo clump while his companions, safe up above, called out superfluous advice: "Run, run, he's trying to catch you!"

The tiger could have taken him in a couple of bounds except that it kept veering wide to make the turn around the clump. Now, my friend was wearing a silk turban, the type that Burmans fancy, and as he went under one bamboo tree, a branch swept the turban from his head. The cloth fell onto the head of the tiger right behind, covering its face, blinding it. The tiger sat down, pawing at this unfamiliar obstruction. Meanwhile, the Burmese hunter came running around the clump full tilt and nearly collided with the tiger, which he thought was still on his heels. The gun was pointed in the right direction. All he had to do was pull the trigger. That saved him, but he did no more tiger shooting. "I practically rode on that tiger's back," he used to say. "Never again."

There's no accounting for the behavior of hunters. A very clever chap came out to hunt with me in 1955, an American, about twenty-seven years old, who later became a professor and already was the model of the absent-minded professor. He was forever searching for things right under his nose. Once we took off our shoes to cross a stream, and he became very excited about the fact that he had lost his until I pointed out that he was carrying them in one hand. Sometimes he would leave pieces of equipment behind; sometimes he would insist on accompanying me on reconnoitering expeditions when he was a hindrance rather than a help. I was afraid that he might get himself killed on a hunt. Actually, he came close to getting me killed.

We were up in Assam near the Brahmaputra River. I built a machan where we could look over a field of long grass to the river some two hundred fifty yards ahead. Off to one side, a little farther away, there was a cattle shed where a Gurkha herdsman took care of the animals. This

Gurkha and I had been in the Burma campaign at the same time, so we did a lot of reminiscing and got to be good friends. When I needed a buffalo for the tiger hunt, he let me have a scrawny one that would do for bait. I staked the buffalo out, got up on the machan with my amateur hunter, and waited.

My companion disturbed me immediately by taking a bottle of pills out of his pocket and swallowing a couple. When I asked the obvious question, he explained, "Caffeine tablets to keep me awake." But they didn't keep him awake —I had to keep nudging him as he dozed off with a gentle snore.

All at once, the buffalo was up on its feet, jerking frantically at the rope binding it to the stake. It had seen the tiger before I did, and the cat had come too close to the machan for me to speak without alerting him. I dug my elbow into the hunter's side, gave a slight gesture toward the tiger with my hand, and nodded my advice to shoot. Before he got the gun to his shoulder, the tiger had made a few feints at the buffalo, got through the defenses of its horns and hoofs, and killed it.

I said, "Fire!" He pulled the trigger. The tiger began to scramble wildly around the clearing, hit but not down. I expected a second shot that never came. "Fire!" I exploded. "Fire!" He didn't obey. He sat there watching while the cat, now aware of our presence, rushed into the grass where we couldn't see it any more. "Why didn't you shoot?" I demanded. He replied, "I don't know." All I could do was shake my head in bewilderment.

We had a wounded tiger to deal with. Early in the morning the Gurkha came out and joined us on the machan. Later a mahout who was helping me with the hunt arrived with an elephant, and we all climbed aboard for a sortie into the grass. After some fruitless combing of the area, the

Gurkha climbed a tree for a look around. He was reporting no sign of the tiger anywhere near when it suddenly poked its head through the grass a few yards away. I fired two quick shots, hitting the tiger, but also causing the elephant to bolt. A low branch struck my shoulder. I did a backward somersault off the elephant, landed in the grass near the cat, flipped over on my side fishing desperately for another cartridge, and somehow managed to load my gun in time for a third shot that did the trick. On the trip home I had trouble being civil to my companion of the hunt.

However, he came back to me in 1961, and I went out with him again. He felt he knew much more about hunting this time, so he insisted on sitting alone near a ford of the Brahmaputra. With a couple of my men, I prepared the area, staking out a goat for bait. We had just finished when he produced a fishing reel, played out a length of line, and said, "Tell your men to tie this to the goat's leg." I inquired what he was about. "If the goat doesn't bleat," he explained, "I'll pull the line and he'll make a sound that will attract the tiger." I tried to tell him that the tiger would discover the goat without assistance, but he insisted on having his way. I had the line tied to the goat's leg, the hunter settled himself to wait with the reel in his hand next to his gun, and I went off and left him.

At about nine o'clock that night I was drinking tea when I heard an unfamiliar sound coming from the Brahmaputra ford, a whirring noise that gave me the feeling something was wrong. I went down with my men to see if the hunter out there was O.K., and along a stretch of the river I saw the body of the goat with the tracks of a tiger around it. From his pug marks, I could tell that he had scrambled up the bank in a big hurry, clearly bothered by something behind him.

We went to the spot where the hunter was waiting. "The

tiger came and grabbed the goat," he said. "He ran with it, and the line began to play out, and the reel was jammed in my hand against the gun. I couldn't get the gun up when the reel was jerked from my hand. It bumped and bounced after the tiger, going 'whirr! whirr!' The tiger ran a little distance with the thing clattering at his heels. Then he dropped the goat and ran away up the bank."

Tigers are easily frightened, especially when they're in a situation that puzzles them. I saw a perfect example of this during World War II.

Since the campaign took place in the jungles of Burma, we overran tiger haunts time after time. Unfortunately, many of them turned into man-eaters because they found so many unburied corpses along jungle trails. Chinese units were badly shot up by the Japanese, they didn't have sufficient medical supplies, and they had to leave the dead where they fell during a retreat. Later hungry tigers came along, had a taste of the corpses, liked the taste, and went from feeding on dead humans to hunting live ones. I would have preferred to shoot these man-eaters whenever we spotted them, but too often that would have alerted the enemy to our position.

On this occasion, the Japanese came and attacked us from one side of a stream, while we held the opposite bank. It was a narrow stream, perhaps thirty feet wide, and the banks were quite steep. We cleared a firing space near a patch of very tall grass, and prepared a hot reception for the enemy. Anyway, the Japanese came through the tall grass, shouting "Banzai!" and firing their rifles. And then there came an unexpected sound from the grass, the loud roar of an angry and frightened tiger. Out he rushed into our cleared space. He got across the river in a headlong scramble and raced down the line past our row of foxholes.

The sight was too much for one of our Kachins, who

stood up and fired at him. The rest of our men forgot the enemy momentarily. They stood up and began taking pot shots at the tiger, who ducked his tail between his legs every time a bullet thudded into the earth behind him. He really ran the gauntlet. Untouched by the flying lead, he galloped into the jungle.

With the tiger out of the way, we went back to our war.

A peaceful tiger came my way once when I was hunting for deer along a stream. I heard a splash as if a heavy object had hit the water, and, walking a little way, I saw a tiger standing in the stream staring down into it. A frog hopped out onto the bank. Like a flash, the tiger pounced on it and gobbled it up. Then he went a little farther, flushed some more frogs, and had them for dinner too. It was an extraordinary sight. You think of the tiger as the monarch of the jungle, killing buffalo and boars and antelope, and here was this one dining on the lowly frog.

Although I thought of shooting him, I was really glad that he turned aside and went away before providing me with a decent target. He must have been either old or injured, no longer capable of catching his usual prey. That made him a prime candidate for man-eater. Instead, he contented himself with frogs. He deserved to get away.

When it comes to the amusing, the comical, the sardonic, the absurd in tiger stories, there's no escaping Sam Barry. I never met Sam Barry, but his story was familiar to everyone in Assam, where he started a new tea estate. He was clearing the jungle so his men could lay out the gardens, but the area was still pretty wild at the time of this incident.

A man-eating tiger had killed a few people in the jungle. One evening a man came to Sam Barry and warned him that the brute had been spotted padding toward his tea estate. He and two of his assistants decided to sit up that night on the veranda of the bungalow and see if the tiger showed itself. The jungle came close enough for them to notice any movement along its fringe. Unfortunately, it came close enough also for a tiger to sneak in right under their noses. He must have known what they were doing, for he slipped around the house and approached from a side where he wasn't expected.

After hours of sentry duty without seeing him, the three men became bored and dozed off. That's what the tiger was waiting for. He bounded onto the veranda, seized Sam by the arm, and started to drag him off. Sam knew that if he struggled, he would be killed right there. He therefore followed the beast, walking in a hunched-over position to prevent his arm from being mangled. At the same time, he called out to the men on the veranda, "I say, if you chaps are going to do something, you'd better hurry up. If he gets me into the jungle, I'm finished!"

They were wide awake by then, needless to say. One of them raced into the bungalow and reappeared with an old-fashioned rifle equipped with a bayonet. He ran after the tiger, plunged the bayonet into his shoulder, and pulled the trigger. The tiger dropped Sam and went after the man with the gun. But the tiger, having suffered a severe injury, couldn't move fast enough. Sam and his two assistants got into the building and barricaded themselves for the night. The next morning they saw the tiger dead on the veranda.

Although that tiger story could stand by itself, it has an extraordinary epilogue. Many years passed, and then I visited a missionary friend of mine, Dr. Pauline Taylor, who was superintendent of St. Luke's Hospital at Chabua in Assam. I mentioned the Barry anecdote, saying that many people I told it to refused to believe it. Miss Taylor then recounted the epilogue: A middle-aged gentleman traveling in England took a train from London to somewhere. Two young chaps sat opposite him in the coach. One was reading a newspaper and suddenly laughed out loud. "Listen to this," he elbowed his companion. "Here's a fantastic, ridiculous story about a planter in Assam being dragged off his veranda by a tiger. Name of Sam Barry. The piece says he simply walked along with the tiger toward the jungle because it had him by the arm. Seems he shouted to an aide to do something, and the bloke got a gun and shot the tiger. Who do they think they're fooling, anyway?"

"Young man, they're not fooling anybody," the middle-aged gentleman interrupted him. "That incident is the gospel truth. You can take it from me. I'm Sam Barry."

7

Witches and
Weretigers

Practically all of the simple village people I knew in Burma, and plenty of sophisticated townsmen as well, had implicit belief in preternatural beings. At home I was taught not to take seriously the belief in magic and witchcraft so prevalent in Southeast Asia. My father considered such things patently false since they clashed with his Christian faith. My mother scoffed at the stories of uncanny spirits inhabiting the jungle and revealing themselves to man in strange mysterious ways.

I stuck to my family training—for the most part. Still, I never could feel quite so positive after I became an experienced jungle man. There were too many things I ran into that seemed beyond explanation in Western terms. When Burmans I respected declared themselves entirely convinced,

I was forced to withhold judgment. Instead of saying no to a story of this or that eerie event, I'd say maybe.

The most widespread Burmese belief in the preternatural concerns the *nats*, spirits inhabiting the household and the forest. The family propitiates the *nats* by setting out food for them with certain prescribed ceremonies. In the jungle a hunter will do the same, setting out coconuts, rice, and cookies flanked by a couple of candles at the foot of a spreading banyan tree, going through the sacred rituals, and saying a brief prayer before departing on the trail of his quarry. If he bags his antelope or pig or leopard, the local explanation is that the *nats* brought the beast within range of his gun.

But there are more tangible representatives of the occult than these animistic spirits. Common Burmese opinion holds that the man eaten by a tiger or killed by a cobra had it coming to him—some crime he committed caused one supernatural being or another to send the deadly creature into his path just in time to strike him down. They are all part of an unseen universe interacting with our ordinary workaday world.

In one village I went out with an elephant hunter who had lived there all his life. We scouted the jungle all morning without finding the rogue we were after. I was damning our bad luck, but my companion just shook his head and said, "We shouldn't be hunting today. Last night there was a full moon. You and I have offended the spirits of the forest." We returned to the village and waited for the full moon to wane before we hunted again.

This business of downing tools at inconvenient moments ranked among the more irritating Burmese customs with the administrators and officers of the British Raj. Astrologers usually determined these days by consulting the signs of the zodiac, drawing up horoscopes, and then plotting lucky and unlucky days on their star charts. Saturday, for instance, was considered unlucky during specific months for those unfortunate enough to be born on that day.

Every month the full moon paralyzed village life throughout Burma. Well up on the occult, the elephant hunter had a fund of stories to beguile me with while we waited for a better lunar phase. From him I heard the tale of Grandmother Red Rock and Grandmother Black Rock, a yarn of witchcraft and wizardry. He assured me Burma has been full of these bizarre arts since the beginning of time.

It seems that in olden days two witches presided over this district. They were good witches, as distinguished from bad witches—a basic distinction to the Burmans—which means that these two old women used their occult powers to keep the villagers on the straight and narrow. By means of spells and incantations they punished the wicked and rewarded the virtuous.

"The two witches dominated our people," my informant stated, "until a wizard came into the area. He too wielded occult powers, and he challenged them for supremacy. The struggle was a mighty one, with each side using sorcery. The wizard won. He turned the witches into stones and placed them in the stream, where you can still see them. The russet-colored stone is Grandmother Red Rock. The dark one is Grandmother Black Rock.

"However, the wizard could not deprive them of all their occult powers. They retain their authority over two king cobras, golden hamadryads, which they send to punish those guilty of wrongdoing. One or two villagers die every year from snake bite, but the others don't worry because they know the victims brought this fate on themselves."

That story made me shudder slightly—and I didn't feel any better later on when I crossed the stream by stepping from Grandmother Red Rock to Grandmother Black Rock.

As I stepped onto the bank, I kept my rifle pointed into the grass. I didn't intend to start an anecdote about myself and the two witches, or be referred to as an object lesson, killed by a king cobra sent to punish me for my sins.

On one of my rounds in the district where I shot elephants, I heard the strangest tale that even a Burmese storyteller could imagine. An old hunter, thoroughly familiar with all the animals of the jungle, started a big sambar—nothing unusual, the kind of stag he had shot dozens of times before. He raised his gun, fired, and hit it in the neck. The sambar dashed away, leaving a trail of blood. The hunter knew his way around the jungle, and, although dusk was falling, he followed the trail with the intention of making a kill. The blood smears led him on to a shallow stream.

As he reached the bank, he heard a human voice around a bend saying, "I told you not to go on that side of the stream." He couldn't make any sense out of the words; all he could think was that someone had found his sambar dead and was about to make off with his venison. Cautiously he walked forward to a point where he could see around the bend—and now he could hear everything plainly.

The sambar was standing in the stream with a piece of cloth tied around its neck. Next to the stag was a man—tall, fair, slightly white beard—who held the end of the cloth in one hand. Bending down, the man scooped water with the other hand, raised it to the sambar's neck, and washed the wound where the hunter's bullet had struck. Addressing the sambar, he said, "I told you not to go on that side of the stream. You make me suffer when you won't listen. You went on that side against my wishes, and now look what has happened to you. Do as I say, and you won't get hurt again. There, I've cleaned your wound. The pain will stop soon. Now we will go where you will be safe."

The man led the sambar out of the water, up the opposite

bank, and into the jungle. The hunter, badly frightened, re-treated hastily to the village. When he recounted what he had seen, the villagers weren't surprised. Several confirmed the story, saying that in their parents' time a mysterious fair man and a big sambar had been seen in the jungle together, and the man had been heard speaking to his companion. "They wander out there forever," said one villager, while the rest nodded in agreement.

The folklore of Burma gives pride of place to the animal that dominates the interest, the imagination, and the fears of the jungle people: tales of the supernatural tiger abound. It's easy to see how this tradition developed. Tigers invade dreams, haunt villages, ambush victims, and outwit pursuers. Add to this a fund of tiger stories about events that puzzle rational explanation, and naturally the big cat gets credited with superhuman cunning as well as diabolical ferocity.

Whenever I'm asked whether a tiger will play with a fawn or a piglet like a cat with a mouse, I tell the one about a young man who went into the jungle to search for some of his cattle. He failed to return. As darkness fell, his mother became extremely agitated. She wept and wailed, and cried out, "A tiger has taken my son!" Her friends attempted to sooth her by predicting he would be back in the morning with a reasonable explanation—namely, that, having been led so far by his straying cows, he decided to spend the night at the next village.

The mother finally went to sleep, but she rose in a flood of tears. Sobbing bitterly, she said she had hardly closed her eyes when she dreamed that she heard her son calling to her in agonized tones, "Mother, a tiger has got me! He's taken me to the clearing at the end of the trail! I'm being tormented! He's cuffed me with his paws until I'm covered with blood! From time to time, he lies down to one side, lets me

97

get up, pounces on me when I've gone a few feet, and knocks me down again!"

The mother listened to her son's voice going on like this for some time. At the end, he shrieked, "Mother, the tiger is tearing me with his fangs! I'm being killed!" The nightmare ended as she woke up in a fit of trembling. "That proves it!" she wept. "I will never see my son again! A tiger has killed him!"

At dawn some men went into the jungle, followed the trail to the clearing, and found all that remained of the young man's body. A tiger had killed and eaten him. Judging from the condition of the remains, they agreed that the tragedy had occurred at the same time that his mother suffered her nightmare.

There was no reason to doubt that the tiger had put him to a cruel and lingering death. The Burmans know that any one of the big cats will do this with a victim, goading it to an attempted escape before killing it. This hasn't happened to a human victim in my experience, but who is to say it never happens? Not the average Burman, certainly.

Westerners could explain the above incident in rational terms, accepting the nightmare as a coincidence, a mother's overheated imagination acting on a reasonable supposition about what had taken place in the jungle. No such simple explanation would do for an incident reported from my home town of Maymyo. A police sergeant named Spears told us schoolboys of one particular man-eating tiger that preyed on people close to the town. Less than a mile away, a camp had been established for coolies doing road work, to improve communications between Maymyo, Mandalay, and other Burmese cities and towns. At night these men would sleep in open *bashas*, just three walls with the fourth side open facing the road. They'd lie down in a line, each on a pallet, covered by a blanket.

They were sleeping thus one night when a tiger entered the *basha*. No one heard him, but he left a trail of ashes from the fireplace outside, and his procedure was evident. He walked down the line of sleeping men, turned around at the end of the line, came back, *seized a worker* in the middle of the line, and carried him out of the *basha* into the jungle. The body was found partially eaten in the compound of the nearest fruit garden. Enough remained to tempt the tiger to return for a second meal.

A warrant officer of the Gurkha Rifles and two of his men sat over the corpse, which was tied down so the tiger couldn't pick it up and get away before they could fire. Around midnight, under a very bright moon, they saw the tiger come down on the opposite side of the hill, cross the road, pass through a hedge, and enter the compound. He stared around the compound, then glared at the corpse, and started toward it.

Suddenly the corpse rose to a half-reclining position on its side and let out a harsh cry of absolute terror. Looking up at the machan, it pointed wildly, imploringly, toward the approaching beast. The three hunters were so terrified that they began to fire frantically into the compound, reloading and shooting until their ammunition was gone. The tiger, untouched, ran off. The corpse lay down again. That's all it was when morning came—a corpse tied down in front of the machan. The warrant officer and his companions swore that the midnight incident occurred exactly as they described it. The British were more skeptical than the Burmans, who had seen too many uncanny things to doubt this one.

The classical Burmese tale of the supernatural tiger is that of the weretiger. The idea is similar to the werewolf, so familiar in the horror stories of the Western world: a man turns into a wolf, and a wolf into a man, under certain conditions; the eating of an exotic plant during a full moon is one

99

condition the moviemakers have specified more often than most of us can remember. I suppose the werewolf is the European version because the wolf was the most savage animal in Europe when the legends took shape. But in Burma and India the wolf meant nothing. The tiger was the worst marauder of the jungle, and so the weretiger became the terrifying example of the man-beast relationship. And this monster has always been taken very seriously in Southeast Asia. Europeans today have little faith in the werewolf. For Burmans and Indians, the weretiger is a real threat to anyone traversing the jungle.

I ran into this legend early in my career, in 1921, shortly after I had joined the Bombay Burmah Trading Corporation. I've already described how the experienced Burmans under my command helped me succeed in the business of getting out the teak timber. They also gave me hints about tracking and shooting that polished my skill as a hunter. And they added to my knowledge of Burmese folklore. I kept fitting my knowledge into the background of general information picked up in the villages of Upper Burma.

Since our timber camp was so far out in the hinterland, and since we had to pay our men regularly, we hired professional soldiers, Gurkhas and Karens, to guard the payroll money. Bandits roamed the jungle, and every so often they'd kill a paymaster in a camp or a courier on the trail and make off with the funds. At my headquarters we maintained a guard of six soldiers by day and six by night, enough of a force to scare off potential raiders.

One of our Gurkhas kept a herd of cows and earned a second salary by supplying us with milk. On a morning inspection of his herd one day, he was appalled to find five of them dead, each horribly mauled by a tiger. When the Gurkha came to me with his sad story, I agreed to round up a beating party and to hold a big tiger hunt. I decided to lead my beaters to the lair. They came from the camp and the village, most of them armed with long Burmese knives. A few carried Burmese crossbows, primitive weapons but effective when they fired poison-tipped arows. One man carried my shotgun. I had my rifle. We started through the jungle.

This was not an ordinary tiger hunt. The beaters were allowed to shoot lesser game on the side to supplement their rations. Every once in a while I'd hear the twang of a crossbow followed by the shout, "That one is mine!" A marksman had hit a deer or a boar or some other edible animal, which he intended to collect on our return. The poison from the arrow would have taken effect by then, and the arrow would identify the owner, and a lucky family or work gang would have meat for dinner.

The first day of the tiger hunt we shot a lot of game, but no tiger. Circling back, we followed the cattle track through some sandy soil that had taken a clear imprint from the hoofs of the animals clip-clopping homeward. They had been shadowed by a huge tiger. His pug marks were enormous—six or seven inches in diameter—with every line sharply cut into the sandy loam.

The first thing a hunter does with a track is to examine it closely so that he'll be able to recognize the animal in the future. With a tiger, you note the four toes—all cats have four toes—and file away in your memory their size, shape, and pattern.

I gazed at this particular track in utter astonishment. Turning to the Burman with me, I exclaimed, "These paw marks have five toes!" He gave me an odd, fearful look and replied, "Yes, don't you know what this means?" I told him I had no idea except that this tiger must be some sort of freak. "No," the Burman said, "this isn't a freak. It isn't a real tiger. It's a man who has turned himself into a tiger.

101

That's why it has the five toes of a man instead of the four toes of a cat."

"Rubbish!" I snorted.

"What I say is true," he declared. "Up in the hills there is a village called Tamandai where the men can turn into tigers. They know the witchcraft and the spells to do it. They know how to become human beings again. The tiger we are following must be a man from Tamandai."

I didn't know what to think. The idea of a weretiger wasn't something I could take to very easily. And yet the five-toed pug marks were there on the ground, plain evidence of something strange about this particular tiger. In any case, I intended to stay on his trail and finish him off before he took any more cows.

The next day of the beat we passed through a village where the headman reported that the tiger had been seen. I ordered the pursuit to continue. We were getting ready again when a woman came out of the jungle and approached me. She looked a sorry sight. Her hair was disheveled, her sarong soiled, her eyes bright as if from fever. To my embarassment, the woman threw herself at my feet.

"Do not shoot the tiger you are hunting," she begged. "That is my son. We come from Tamandai. He turned himself into a tiger and went off into the jungle. I've been following him for over a month, carrying this bundle of his clothes. All I have to do is drop the bundle in front of him and he'll be himself again, and I'll take him home."

She started to cry. The Burmese started to mutter. They absolutely refused to chase the tiger any further. The woman picked herself up, dried her tears, and vanished into the jungle. The tiger was never seen again.

All the stories of the occult I've related amount to so much child's play when compared to one told to me by a Burman whom I knew to be sober, straightforward, and honest—by no means the type to pull one's leg. However one may judge this part of his autobiography, he certainly was not lying to me.

In his youth he worked as a messenger for the Bombay Burmah Trading Corporation, carrying letters, orders, and other documents between timber camps. He therefore held a fairly responsible position, one granted to him only after his superiors had made a careful investigation of his character and intelligence. They could not afford to have him lose a contract or ignore a timetable or disobey instructions. By appointing him a company messenger they testified to their high opinion of him.

Usually he traveled the jungle trails alone. This time, as he was preparing to leave one camp for another he was asked to wait for another chap, a feller of teak trees, who wanted to go through the jungle to the next camp. The messenger felt happy enough to have a companion on the trek. He delayed until the feller arrived, and although they were late setting out, the messenger felt little concern since two men would be fairly safe even in the jungle at night.

They left the camp, gained the trail, and walked at a good pace, conversing all the while about the company, the teak business, their villages, and their families. They covered many miles, reached a hill overlooking a stream with scrub, grass, and bushes on either bank, and began to descend the hill. They were walking and talking when they heard a lot of squealing up ahead.

"Pigs!" the feller exclaimed. The messenger shrugged and answered, "Yes, pigs. But we might as well forget them. You don't have a gun, and neither do I. There's nothing we can do about it."

They walked a little farther side by side. Again the squealing sounded loudly through the bushes. Now the feller became very excited. "Pigs!" he fairly shouted. The messenger couldn't understand his companion's attitude. "Yes," he responded, "that's a herd of wild pig, as we both know. But there's no use stopping. We have no way of making a kill, and we don't want to be caught in the jungle any later than necessary. Come on!"

"No!" The feller had stopped. He was standing there motionless, breathing hard, his eyes narrowed, his head canted toward the place where the pigs were foraging. "We don't need a gun," he rasped. "Don't ever tell anyone you saw me do this. But, I'll turn into a tiger, and go and kill a pig, and we'll have pork to eat."

The messenger stared in consternation at his companion. Before he could say anything, the feller went on. "Quick! Climb this tree! I'm going to turn into a tiger! You'd better be safely out of reach!"

The messenger didn't know whether to believe the warning or not. Taking no chances, he pulled himself onto a branch as rapidly as he could. "Here, take my clothes," said the feller, as he stripped naked, bundled his garments, and handed them up. "Now climb higher," he said. "When I'm a tiger, I'll be able to jump that high! Go up to where you'll be safe!" Properly terrified, the messenger started climbing and didn't stop until he reached the highest branch that would hold him. He felt cold and clammy as he gazed down at his companion.

"Listen carefully," the feller continued, "or it will be the worse for you. When I get back, I'll be a tiger. You drop my clothes in front of me. When I see them, I'll be myself again. If you don't drop the bundle, I'll be a tiger forever. And the first thing I'll do is wait for you to climb down."

Having said this, the man threw himself down in the mud, where he proceeded to roll over and over. His body began to lengthen. His head flattened and pulled down toward his neck. A tail appeared. His voice changed from the puffs and

104

grunts of a human being to feline growls and snarls. The rolling ceased. Before the messenger's eyes, a tiger rose to its feet and stalked into the jungle.

The horrid experience of seeing his comrade of the teak camp transformed into a tiger left the messenger with no alternative. He clung to the topmost boughs of the tree; his heart thumped in his chest like a drum, and his breath came in short gasps.

He could hear the herd of pigs milling around. Presently there came the clatter of hoofs as the herd stampeded in all directions through the underbrush. One pig began to squeal in agony, the high-pitched screams that indicated some predator had seized it. The squealing cut off. Silence reigned. In the dusk, the messenger could see the waving of the grass tops as a big animal pushed through past the stems below in the direction of the tree. The last rows of grass parted, and a tiger came out into the open. It was the same tiger that had left a few minutes before—the weretiger.

The beast moved forward. He padded nervously back and forth, circled the tree several times, and went back into the grass. Returning, he resumed his padding as if he were waiting for something. Finally he looked up expectantly at the man in the tree.

The messenger had been sitting on his perch, his arms wound tightly around the trunk of the tree, forgetful of everything else. The tiger's look jolted him. Hastily he threw the bundle of clothes to the ground. It landed amid a puff of dust right in front of the tiger, which at once lay down in the mud and began to roll as before. His body diminished. His head took a more rounded form. His tail vanished. The growls of the big cat gave way to human words. A man rose to his feet and began to dress. It was the teak feller.

Fully dressed, he stood with his feet apart and his hands on his hips and addressed the messenger. "I've killed a pig!

Come on down! We'll carry as much as we can to the camp, and we'll have a good meal of pork! Come on down!"

The messenger shook his head. "Not me! I'm staying where I am. You can do what you like with your pig!" The tiger-man looked annoyed. "Then," he said, "I'll come up and join you." This was the last thing the messenger wanted—to be trapped at the top of a tree with a weretiger beneath him—so he climbed down.

"Come on!" the feller said. "Let's go get the pig I killed!" He turned in that direction, expecting the messenger to follow him.

The messenger whipped out his dah, his Burmese knife. "I don't want your pig!" he grated, pointing the dah at the weretiger. "And I'll tell you what we're going to do. You're going to walk along the trail to the next camp, with me right behind you. Stick to the trail, keep going, and don't look back. One false move, and you're a dead man. I'll lop your head off!"

That's how they continued their trek, a forced march for the weretiger at knife point. At the camp, the messenger forced the feller into a hut at one end while he spent a sleepless night in a different hut keeping his knife in his hand and his eyes wide open in case of a visit from his erstwhile companion.

The next morning the messenger heard how the feller had told the rest of the men in his hut about a tiger killing a pig in the jungle and leaving it there uneaten. Burmans never leave such a report unanswered. Enthusiastically they got an elephant, went out under the feller's guidance, and brought the carcass back to camp. As the messenger said to me in recounting the story, "They little realized they had the tiger on the elephant with them!"

This Burman spoke matter-of-factly about what he had seen, as if he were reporting an ordinary boar hunt, except for the undercurrent of tension in his voice that showed how shaken he had been. He pointed out that, for all the were-tiger tales he had heard since his youth, only this once had he ever watched an individual going through the transformation from man into beast and back into man again. But that admission is not unusual in Burma. Nobody pretends to have had frequent experience of the weretiger, and most Burmans live their whole lives without ever encountering the monster.

Defending their belief, they claim to have heard too many eye-witness reports by reputable people. Besides, there are, they will tell you, certain clues that may give away a man's most carefully guarded secret. If he has a scar on his body where a tiger was injured—a bullet wound across the shoulder, perhaps—suspicion will arise that the two are one and the same being under different guises. Or, if a man has a habit of disappearing into a tiger-infested jungle at dusk when everyone else is hurrying home for safety, and if he returns in the morning worn and tired, but looking satisfied from a nighttime feast, those who know him may begin giving him peculiar looks.

This is a frightening thing to have happen in a village, and various ways have been worked out for dealing with it. You don't just go up to a man and say, "Look here, old boy, you're giving us all a bit of the jitters with this tiger stunt. Why not be yourself?" Burmese villagers would shudder at the thought of what he might do. They appeal to his better nature, so to speak. Assuming he becomes a tiger because he isn't satisfied with what he finds at home or in the village, they allow him to have the best of everything. A peaceful wife, quiet obedient children, good meals, friendly neighbors, a place of honor at village feasts, dances, and hunts—these are basic ingredients of the antiweretiger recipe. If the recipe doesn't work, the village chief may go to a professional wizard for a magic potion, a charm, or a spell. Failing that, I suppose the only thing to do with a weretiger is live with him; at least, I've never heard of a man-beast being hunted down and killed after the fashion of the European werewolf or vampire.

I don't pretend to understand the psychology of the weretiger, but presumably it's possible to live with one because familiar surroundings cause him to remain a man. It's usually when he wanders off by himself that he turns into a big cat. In such cases, a wife or mother will wait for him to return as a man, or she may go out after him, as in the story of the woman of Tamandai.

Do I take this manifestation of the occult seriously? My answer is negative. But, because of the strange things I've seen in Burma, I'm not going to ridicule the Burmans who believe in the weretiger.

8

Cornered by
the King Cobra

If I were living permanently in a house in a Burmese village, and if I had to choose just one animal for a pet, I would take the mongoose. This is a delightful little creature, grayish in color, weighing some three pounds, possessed of a bushy tail at one end and a sharp intelligent face with bright eyes at the other. Easily tamed, a mongoose will romp around a house like a frisky kitten or a pup, or ride on your shoulder as you putter about the yard.

I have another reason for my choice. I hate snakes, and if you keep a mongoose, you don't have snakes in the house. A mongoose specializes in challenging the most horrendous denizen of the jungle, the king cobra. And that's enough for me.

I've often watched an Indian snake charmer putting on an

act with a mongoose and a cobra, bringing the snake out of a basket and allowing the mongoose to have a go at it until it becomes tired enough to get hurt. Then the cobra goes back into the basket, while the spectators who have gathered around pet the mongoose and toss a few coins to the snake charmer.

I've seen only one real fight to the death between a cobra and a mongoose. I was in an Assamese tea garden on a very hot day at about three in the afternoon, relaxing after a jungle patrol, when I noticed a quick movement in the bushes across the compound. A mongoose was hovering around the edge of the bushes, peering intently into them. He would start in suddenly, and stop, and back away in a constant play of spasmodic motion. Now he would be crouched down on four legs; now he would rise up on two legs. Always his sharp little eyes remained fixed on that spot in the bushes. A pattern of activity soon became obvious. The mongoose would run forward a little less each time, and he would draw back a little more, gradually moving into the open area of the compound on my side of the bushes. After him came a king cobra eight or nine feet long.

The mongoose had maneuvered it out into the open. He had discovered the snake in the bushes, and by goading it, barely within reach, barely beyond reach, had tempted it to strike repeatedly. Since a cobra rears about one-third of its length off the ground, its weight brings it a little forward after a lunge. Without realizing what was happening, the snake abandoned the security of the bushes, advancing into the compound, where the mongoose had some fighting room.

Now began the classical battle of the mongoose and the cobra. The animal worried the snake by pretending to attack, by feinting and dodging and scooting from one side to the other, within range when the snake was deciding to strike, out of range when it did strike. The cobra would lunge, miss,

110

and hit the ground with a thump. The mongoose would dart in boldly, skip aside, circle around, and come in at a different angle. His agility made the difference. His movements were like lightning compared to those of the cobra. It was an extraordinary sight, this small animal, the size of a squirrel, baiting an enormous snake armed with sufficient venom to destroy him in a few seconds.

I noticed that the cobra was becoming tired. It struck more slowly than when the battle began. It had more difficulty rearing back into an upright position. Baffled, outwitted, it faced an antagonist that seemed to gain in stamina and determination. The snake struck for the last time. Before it could raise its head, the mongoose flashed into close quarters and seized it by the back of the neck in a death grip. The snake writhed as the sharp teeth crunched together at the base of the skull. When it lay still, the mongoose dragged it back into the bushes for a meal.

One evening I was hunting jungle fowl when dusk was falling and they were fluttering into the trees to roost. They made a lot of rustling noises, beating their wings and flicking their tails, and, guided by the sound, I went on until I saw a hen on the ground run around a bush. I followed as quietly as possible. What sounded like a hen calling gave me a lead. Moving onward, reaching the place where the sound was coming from, I heard a rustling on the ground, looked down, and saw a hamadryad making the sound. It sounded exactly like a jungle fowl. Whether it could have lured a bird close enough for a kill, I don't know—and I shot it without learning. The king cobra can also imitate the call of a pheasant.

My worst cobra confrontation occurred when I was after a rogue elephant in the jungle alongside some tea estates in Assam, near the Himalayas. One morning I heard the breaking of branches and the noise of an elephant feeding, so I went out with my rifle. This turned out to be the wrong elephant, and I left him alone. Disappointed, I continued into the jungle hoping to find a tiger. Later I returned to the tea estate entrance intending to go to my room.

Grass five or six inches high had overgrown the path, making visibility underfoot difficult. Carrying my rifle in my left hand, I walked down a slope, made a turn around a bend, and heard a rough rustling sound that seemed to sweep along the ground toward me. Startled, I swung around just in time to see a huge king cobra, at least twelve feet long, rear into a striking position. Probably it had been basking in the sun, started to retreat, and then felt I was about to step on its tail. Anyway, the snake changed its mind in a split second. Instead of slithering off, it swept back like a flash—the rustling sound that drew my attention—and assumed its attack stance before I was aware of its presence.

The hamadryad was close enough to hit me in the ribs if it decided to strike. Instinct told me to freeze in my tracks. I was cornered. If I had started to raise my rifle, I would have been bitten long before I could get it into position for a shot. If I attempted to run, the snake would have sunk its fangs into my back or my leg before I had taken a step. I would have died agonizingly, as do so many people in Southeast Asia who are bitten by the hamadryad every year.

This horrible creature, its hood spread wide, swayed gently from side to side. I was afraid to blink and prayed I wouldn't lose my nerve and panic, as I looked into those chilling eyes. We stood there trying to stare each other down. To my unspeakable relief, the cobra gave in. It stopped swaying, lowered its head into the grass, and slithered away into the underbrush. As it went, I could hear the birds and squirrels scolding in each tree it passed. I reached my room in a cold sweat after one jungle experience I don't care to recall.

Another impromptu meeting with a hamadryad occurred when I was showing a party of hunters how to track a wounded deer through the jungle. After giving them some instructions, I let them go on without me so they could have the thrill of the kill, and I sat down on a log to wait. Everything was bone-dry—the log, the bushes, the grass, the earth. I was wiping the sweat off my forehead when I heard a distinct rustling in the grass behind me, a sound too loud to be made by a breeze—and there was no breeze. A movement caught my eye. Turning my head, I saw a cobra gliding down toward the end of the log. I guessed that it had been asleep in the dry grass and had been jarred when I sat down on the log.

When the hamadryad reached the end of the log, it pulled about half of its length into a coil, doubled back up onto the log, and advanced toward where I sat, ten feet away. It came very slowly, inch by inch, watching me with a fixed stare as if it wanted to know more about the strange creature who had disturbed its nap in the sun. Ordinarily I would have leapt to one side and shot the snake.

This time I sat where I was. The behavior of this cobra interested me—I'd say we interested each other. Moreover, my shotgun was lying across my knees pointing directly at it, so all I had to do was pull the trigger. I had buckshot in the left barrel and ball in the right. Which to use? I debated the question in my mind. The buckshot seemed the poorer choice since it scatters when it leaves the muzzle, and I thought the pellets might spray around the snake's head instead of hitting it directly. On the other hand, I didn't want to use ball because it was a single bullet and might miss altogether. There was a third choice in my ammunition belt, the number-eight cartridge we used for shooting jungle fowl on the wing. The three hundred pellets of small shot would certainly score enough hits to mangle the snake.

Very gingerly, imitating the slow caution of the advancing cobra, I put my hand down to my belt. Fumbling with my fingers while keeping my eyes on it, I lifted a number-eight shot cartridge, opened the breech of the gun, expelled the ball, slipped the number-eight in, and closed the gun.

Despite the extreme care of my actions, my movements told the cobra that it faced a living thing on the log. It began to spread and close its hood as a cobra will when disturbed or angry. Spreading and closing, spreading and closing, it came up the log. Slowly I raised the gun, got a bead on the snake's head, and our eyes met along the sights. A slight squeeze of the trigger, and I could have torn the creature apart.

The hamadryad must have felt instinctively that some kind of danger threatened it up the log. Twisting its head to one side, it started to glide off at right angles, to the rear, back where it had emerged from the grass. It still refused to hurry. Methodically, inch by inch, it coiled off the log, apparently with the intention of creeping silently away. Half the length had gone over the log when I fired. The blaze of pellets severed the snake completely in two, its upper half falling behind the log, its lower half in front. I opened the gun and replaced the number-eight with ball again, thinking that the incident was over. The only problem was to deal with the deer, which, as I feared, dashed away as the sound reverberated through the jungle. I heard a voice yelling, "He's gone back! He's gone back!" The hunters weren't happy about having their deer scared off. They ran up demanding to know why I had fired.

"Look on the other side of the log and you'll see why," I replied. We all looked. I could hardly believe my eyes. Instead of the snake thrashing around in its death throes, the upper half had gone down along the log through the leaves and grass, just as it had when it was whole and I had first noticed it. At the end of the log, it turned again to mount the log and move up toward me. It tried its best. Having lost its steering apparatus—its tail, which lay on the other side of the log—the cobra rolled and pitched out of control, the head unable to direct what was left of the body.

During one rainy season when I was with the Bombay Burmah Trading Corporation, we were living in *bashas* as usual. My *basha* was of purely functional construction, without unnecessary additions. Instead of rising to the ceiling, the walls terminated some four feet off the floor, and they enclosed only three sides. The fourth side lay open, and from it a flight of three or four steps extended to the ground. The bed was on one side of the *basha,* in a corner. This arrangement gave me all the comfort I needed, keeping the rain out and allowing me to free myself from the mud by kicking off my boots when I entered.

One day after lunch I was lying on the bed in the *basha,* snug and dry despite the deluge of rain splattering on the roof and pouring down the eaves. With our work well in hand, I could afford a break. Although my shotgun was leaning against the corner post at the head of the bed, ready in case I needed it, I didn't expect to need it very soon. Not a sound reached my ears except the patter of raindrops. The whole camp had relaxed for an early-afternoon siesta.

I was absorbed in a book, *The Scarlet Pimpernel,* Baroness Orczy's exciting historical novel about the English gentleman who rescued people from the guillotine during the French Revolution. Every now and then I'd turn my eyes away from the book and look at the beautiful paddy fields down below with the paddy growing knee-high, looking like the top of a billiard table, smooth and green. After a glance, I would turn back to the novel, resuming the adventures of the Scarlet Pimpernel.

By degrees, a strange feeling crept over me, an irritation I couldn't explain, a mental block that prevented me from concentrating. I tried to shake the mood off and read on. I put the book down; I picked it up; I repeated the same performance a moment later. Something was wrong, but I couldn't put my finger on it.

Suddenly another sensation came over me. I recognized it as the familiar experience of gaining somebody's attention by fixing your gaze on the back of his head. It may be in a church or in a bus, but if you stare at him with unswerving concentration, the moment will come when he will turn around and look at you. I've known this to happen when I tried it with my friends. That was the sensation that stirred me as I lay on the bed in the *basha*. I put my book down, turned my head to the wall of the *basha* beside me, and saw a huge snake draped over the low wall, its snout not more than two feet from my ear. It was staring over my shoulder as if it too had been following the story.

I was terror-stricken. Somehow, with a burst of muscular energy that I didn't know I had, I hopped off the bed onto the floor, crawled along to the open end of the *basha,* and rolled down the steps to the ground outside. I yelled to my boys, "Come over here! There's a big snake in my *basha!*" Naturally, the snake got just as much of a fright as I did. It slithered up from the wall into the thatch of the roof, trying to find some way of escape.

As I saw it go, I crawled back into the *basha.* Stooping down and glancing up, I grabbed my shotgun and ran out. By then the snake was crawling along in the thatch, and the nearest members of the teak timber corps had arrived. I shouted to them, "Throw stick and stones at it! Make it come out where I can get a shot!" Missiles bounced off the roof near the snake, which abandoned the thatch for an overhanging tree, perhaps the one that had given it an access route down into the *basha.* As it slid from one branch to another, I shot it in the head. The creature fell to the ground, twisted convulsively, and lay still.

Cornered by the King Cobra

These encounters with snakes were among my most terrifying moments. Creatures like these are enough to keep you on edge. In the dense jungle, I'd rather face a man-eating tiger or a rampaging boar or a charging elephant. It's easier to see the big game, easier to hit them; and they don't leave you feeling slightly nauseated, quite the contrary. I love the four-footed animals, however dangerous. I will never love a snake.

9

In Flight from the Japanese

My career as a jungle man spanned more than half a century. Telling about it, I've moved around through the decades and across hundreds of miles of territory, introducing some tigers I've known, and elephants, and other big game of Burma, without pausing to date each incident. Where stories of the same type belong together, I've put them together—all snakes in one chapter, for instance, although I met them many years apart. However, the great division in my life wouldn't make sense apart from the time sequence.

I mean World War II.

By then two things had happened that changed everything for me: I had gotten married, and I had shaken the dust of the Bombay Burmah Trading Corporation from my boots.

My wife was a Maymyo girl who lived not far from our house with her mother and sister. She and I had a lot in common, as she liked shooting. We'd often go out together after duck in the marsh or along the shores of a pond, and we'd make forays into the jungle for deer or wild pig. She was more inclined to city ways than I was, and we paid regular visits to Mandalay by car. Occasionally we made the longer trip to Rangoon and stayed in my mother's flat—she lived there permanently now, since her children were grown. As lively as ever, she still made the rounds of the Burmese capital to see her relatives, enjoyed having her sons and daughters drop in on her, and presided over the family gatherings on holidays. She was as energetic as any of us. At the age of eighty-four, she trekked out of Burma ahead of the Japanese invasion, and made her way to Manipur in India and then to Lahore in what is now Pakistan.

I didn't see as much of my wife during our years of marriage as I would have liked. After I went into elephant control, I was away from home fifty-one weeks out of the year. The arrival of our son cut into her leisure, especially when he grew old enough to attend school in Maymyo. My shift to the ruby-mine area of Burma allowed us more time together, for they were able to come and stay in camp with me during the winter months. We'd do some tracking and shooting and have a good time before they had to return home. But obviously my work separated me from my family for long periods.

At the time of our marriage I was staying in Maymyo. I had just finished with the timber company because I couldn't get on with the pukka sahibs any longer; they seemed to be scraping the bottom of the barrel for new men to send out from England. One of these assistants irritated me so much that I told him off and resigned. Whereupon they made things rough by spreading the word and getting me blacklisted. I couldn't even find a job. I tried my luck at running pigs from upcountry down to Mandalay, and my luck was good until a Burman I trusted skipped off with the pigs and the profits.

Then I managed to get another timber job with a small firm run by an Indian proprietor who needed men willing to work under difficult conditions. Things were changing "out East," with anti-British feeling running high; and of course the Indians, being foreigners in Burma, and associated with imperial rule, faced the same kind of resentment. Most districts were affected. Up and down the Irrawaddy bandits and rebels moved through the countryside almost at will, aided and abetted by the villagers. An individual who called himself the rightful King of Burma attracted a following and started the so-called Tharrawaddy Rebellion, in which some British forest officers were killed, one being shot to death while taking a bath.

The violence became so bad that the man who should have been in charge of timber operations refused to go in there. The Indian proprietor asked me to go, and I said I would and I did. He offered me a commission of one rupee on every log I brought out. Since there were more than thirty thousand logs, this meant an income too substantial to turn down, even with the danger involved. I had no intention of being a hero, much less a martyr; I knew this part of Burma and its people and felt quite sure that I could handle both.

When my acceptance became known, the regular officer who had balked came to the company headquarters with a complaint. He insisted he'd been ready to go all along, but he required a bodyguard. As an old-timer who had put in years with the organization, he had the ear of the owner, who agreed to foot the bill for a file of Indian military police to accompany him. I said that a couple of experienced jungle men would be enough and that so many would only attract attention. The man remained stubborn, got what he wanted, and, when we reached the Tharrawaddy District, we had to set up a big camp, where he himself took up residence in a *basha* he called "my palace."

We saw so many signs of rebel activity that I wondered whether his "palace" might not be stormed some night. I still think he was lucky this never happened. During this period I had something to do with keeping the rebels off balance. A wild Gurkha, eager for more action than he could find in the camp, came to me one day and said, "Let's you and me go out in the morning and see if we can get some rebels. Between us we can knock out a few!" The situation in camp had become so bad I figured I had little to lose. So we went out and scoured the jungle. We had some shooting affairs after that first day, and on one occasion we entered a bandit camp evacuated so recently the fire was smoking and gear lay all around. We returned from this foray with quite a haul of rice.

When word of our exploit got back to headquarters, the boss didn't like it at all. Much of his gripe was simply the old Indian-Burman antagonism, and this now more heated than ever. He feared the Burmans of the Tharrawaddy District would say, "Your man killed some Burmans. We're going to drive your work gangs out, kill your elephants, and burn your timber." Afraid that his operation might collapse. He told me to go. I went.

It was soon afterward that I got into the elephant control division of the Game Department, where I was when the Japanese invasion hit Burma.

Until then, there had been little concern over Japanese expansion in the Far East. Whatever happened in China

seemed far away. In any case, the Burmans didn't sym-
pathize with the Chinese, whom they resented in Burma
as too successful businessmen. Up in Maymyo we assumed
that the Japanese would never get that far. Out in the
villages a complete fatalism prevailed as far as the political
situation went, the people being quite prepared to accept
whichever imperial power came out on top, and many
preferred the rule of Orientals to that of Europeans. Some
even believed the Japanese would do Burma a favor by
driving out the Chinese, the Indians, and the British.

When the invasion came, probably the only thing agreed
upon was that the Japanese moved faster than anyone
thought possible. It was the same story as in Malaya: the
idea that the enemy would find the jungle too tough to
penetrate with an army proved ridiculously untrue. The
Nipponese columns smashed into Burma and fanned out in
different directions. They moved so fast that no place, however remote, looked safe. Up in Maymyo, we soon stopped
saying, "The Japanese will never reach us." Instead, we
prepared to get out while there was still time.

I had just delivered a cargo of ivory in Maymyo, when I
received an order to proceed to Moulmein, where my immediate assignment would be to examine new timber from
different sawmills and classify the best as war supplies.
When I got to Moulmein, in southeastern Burma on the
Salween, I found myself right in the path of the Japanese
invasion. The people of Moulmein were convulsed with
fear and uncertainty. The invaders were approaching the
city. Disloyal Burmans were guiding them. Rumors like
those fed the panic. People milled around, wondering what
to do.

I had my first experience of shooting war one morning
when I walked along a ridge outside Moulmein, and heard
roaring, shrieking, whining noises up in the sky. Two small

planes were dueling, diving at each other, zooming off, and trying to gain altitude. The sound of machine guns echoed faintly on the morning air. The planes flew off. Returning to Moulmein, I reported what I had seen to my friend Bodeker, a timber expert. He looked grave. "The Japanese must be getting near if their planes are flying over Moulmein. We'd better get our things together and be ready to leave."

We went down to the river, toward the jetty, to see what we could find out. Some troops of the Burma army were headed in the same direction. I saw a friend of mine, asked what the situation was, and received the warning: "The Japanese are coming up. We're going to form a defense line along the river and try to save Moulmein, but I don't think we have enough men, and you'd better get out while you can. No one knows what's going to happen."

Back in Moulmein, everyone in the timber industry was in a frenzied uproar. The sawmill owners wanted one thing: to clear out as much of their stock as possible as fast as possible. They were passing out money by the basketful. One implored me, "Here's ten thousand rupees. Take them. You can use them when you reach India. Only pass my timber!" Other timber men offered as much as fifteen thousand rupees. Sometimes I regret refusing these bribes—other people took the money, carried it to Calcutta, and lived well during the war.

Just as my friend had feared, the British-Burmese line along the Sittang River broke when the Japanese smashed into the undermanned defenses. Somebody ordered a bridge blown up prematurely, trapping thousands of men on the opposite side of the river. The Japanese came on and on, brushing aside all opposition, and poured into Moulmein. Before they got there, I received instructions to go north and continue my timber work. However, it obviously

124

couldn't continue much longer. Burma was cracking up under the Japanese blows. Enemy columns pushed toward Rangoon and through the jungle. Hordes of refugees fled before them, desperately attempting to reach safety in India to the west.

The first thing I now did was hurry north to Maymyo, to pick up my family. I intended to take them to Mandalay, where they could get a plane to India. But Mandalay had just been heavily bombed, so I put them on a train to Myitkyina in north Burma, where the airfield was still open and a plane for India was waiting, reserved for old people, women, and children—no able-bodied men. I never saw my wife and son again.

Later I heard how they were delayed from day to day in Myitkyina, until May 6, 1942, when they were on the airstrip waiting for a plane along with a group of other refugees. Japanese fighter planes came down and machine-gunned the airstrip. Among the casualties were my mother-in-law and one of her daughters. A second girl, wounded in the head by a bomb splinter, later died of her injury. The Japanese pilots zipped off, leaving the mangled bodies of women and children scattered across the Myitkyina airstrip. Eventually my wife and son, with her injured sister, joined a trek to Sumprabum in the tribal area of the Kachins. The idea was to reach Indian Assam through the Hukawng Valley.

The tea planters of Assam had formed organizations to go out and meet the people trying to escape from Burma. These rescue operations saved a lot of people, but a lot more never got through because Burma has so many swift rivers and streams. There weren't enough men and boats to get women and children across the deeper channels. The refugees who made for the shallower places often underestimated the strength of the current and were swept away. Pitifully few ever made it. And those who did congregated pathetically on the riverbanks without food or change of clothing or protection from the elements, and one by one they died of malaria, hunger, or exposure while waiting for help that never came.

The villagers, country people, who set out for India had a better chance of survival than the others. They were used to the jungle, and they knew how to live in it. The city people lacked that kind of experience. Later, when I went through the area with Merrill's Marauders, I saw traces of the harrowing ordeal they suffered. They had tried to build shelters; the mute witnesses were thin little saplings, about six feet tall, stuck in the ground with blankets tied at the top for a sort of square roofing. Sometimes blankets on the ground covered skeletons, the last remains of the weary, the sick, and the injured who huddled there until death put an end to their suffering. Here and there a rotting scarf or handkerchief revealed the last of the personal belongings they had tried to salvage from the wreckage of war. I felt desolated by the sight even though I was used to death by that time.

Having seen my family off on the train to Myitkyina, I returned to Maymyo to see if I could help anybody else. No timber work remained to be done. The situation had become too chaotic for anything except a dash west—if we were to escape the Japanese. I joined the long lines of refugees making for the Chindwin River.

The last refugees from Maymyo included a number of my relatives—a brother-in-law who was a registrar of the high court, a niece, her sister and three children. Several friends joined our party, as did a couple of soldiers of the garrison who volunteered to drive a military truck to Shwebo. I thought they were doing us a favor, until they stopped the truck near the courthouse and announced they were leaving. An officer suddenly arrived in a jeep with a sergeant, arrested them for being beyond their jurisdiction, and took them away—with the keys to the truck. I had all these women and children, plus some rather ineffectual men, on my hands, and there we were stranded in Shwebo. Fortunately, a mechanic knew how to start the truck motor with a piece of wire. We piled back into the vehicle, which I drove fifty miles to Monywa on the Chindwin. Monywa seemed a madhouse, with refugees scrambling along the river, desperate for any kind of transportation to the other bank. Small boats of all types were in constant motion back and forth, like swarms of waterflies on the surface of the river.

I decided to spend the night before crossing and led the way to the home of a priest. He gave us a hail-and-farewell greeting: "Welcome, welcome, but *I'm* off tonight! You can have the bungalow!" His attitude was typical. The Japanese were already in the vicinity and would catch up with anyone who didn't move quickly.

The next morning, as luck would have it, a launch belonging to an old schoolmate of mine came chugging along and stopped where we were. He said he was taking his family to a point upriver where a clear road led to Manipur, in Assam, and that he could take most of my party aboard. However, I myself and a couple of other men had to find other means of reaching India. That suited me. The launch went off, we looked around for another boat, and got across the Chindwin in a dugout. I was now in familiar territory where I had hunted elephants. The hills gave me a feeling of nostalgia. Some of the happiness of the earlier days touched me despite the changed conditions.

I was prepared to make the trek upstream along the bank, but the others were city chaps who couldn't make it on foot, and so I told the boatman we'd pay him well to row

127

us to our destination. He promised he would. Then he brought his boat ashore on the opposite bank—at Kyauk Hmaw village, eight miles diagonally across from Monywa— with the excuse that he had to go off for rations. He came back, only to keep us stuck there on the grounds that his oarsman was sick and couldn't row. He went off again. His behavior would have made anyone suspicious. I judged that he intended to hold us there while he met the Japanese advance guard and alerted them to where we were. My suspicion was vindicated when guns opened fire on the area and at Monywa, as the enemy was obviously trying to kill any refugees they couldn't catch. It was a terrible sight: frightened people milling around in the gloom as shells crunched and exploded.

I didn't wait for any more evidence that we were in the hands of a Burmese quisling. I sent my companions to a Buddhist monastery beyond which the trail extended west, with the intention of following immediately and catching up. A slight interruption occurred at this point. A Japanese pilot surveying the area for targets spotted me and zoomed down firing his guns. Jumping onto the bank, I sprinted under a broad mango tree. The pilot flew so low I could see his goggles before he swerved off.

I ran up to the monastery. My companions had vanished down the trail, and, as I reached the other side of the grounds, a group of Burmans barred my way. One charged, "You're wearing muddy boots. You're not supposed to be stepping on the sacred earth of the monastery." They confronted me with surly expressions. What they wanted was unmistakable: the two guns I carried. In no mood to be trifled with, anxious to get on with the trek to India, I snapped, "Look, I'm in a hurry. I have no time to argue." I raised my shotgun and went on through. Reaching the road, I turned and said to them, "I'm off sacred ground now.

If you follow me, I'll shoot you." They began to whine and wheedle, insisting they were willing to pay for my firearms. I gave them a blunt no and went to the nearest trail, which was full of refugees on the march.

Traveling by day and night, on foot and by boat, along highways and through back jungles, picking up companions en route, including the husband of my older sister, I made it to the Indian border.

In Calcutta I stowed my things in a boarding house and went twice a day to inquire about the latest refugees from Burma at the Loreto Convent, where the homeless people were taken to be looked after. Every morning and every evening I would ask if my family had arrived, and each time I received a negative reply. No news of them ever came.

At first my feelings were numb, but as hope ran out I became increasingly bitter toward those responsible. The Japanese had caused me personal tragedy. They had created a refugee problem in which the sufferings of those who escaped brought home more starkly the fate of those who failed to get through from Burma. The enemy had thrown the crushing weight of an army of occupation upon my country, and their generals now ran Pegu, my birthplace, and Maymyo, my home. They had turned my life into a shambles.

Gradually a passion for revenge took possession of me. I longed to even the score with the Mikado's men, and eventually I did, with infinite satisfaction.

10

Five Hundred
Rupees and a
Bag of Salt

When the Japanese put a price on my head, I didn't know
a thing about it. All I knew at the time was that I was
fighting the soldiers from Nippon in the jungle, doing my
best to see that as few of them as possible got away in one
piece. My first campaign against them was over and done
with before I learned in a roundabout way of the compli-
ment the invaders of Burma had paid me.

I was recuperating at a military rest area in Shillong,
Assam. We used to take our meals four at a table, and I
noticed an officer at another table glancing in my direction
every so often. Finally he came over and addressed me. "Are

131

you Captain Girsham?" "I am," I answered, "but who are you?" He identified himself as Jock Stuart Jones of the Gurkha Rifles. Recently when he was being released from St. Luke's Hospital in Chabua, the matron suggested that he get in touch with a former patient, now in Shillong—me.

"I was one of General Orde Wingate's men," Jock Stuart Jones explained. "We had to retreat through the jungle. When we reached Bhamo District, a chief told us to go down by way of N' Sop Zup in the Sumprabum area, where we'd meet a certain Captain 'Kassim.' That was how he pronounced your name; he couldn't say 'Girsham' properly. The chief added that this Captain 'Kassim' and his Kachins were fighting so successfully that the Japanese had put a price on his head—five hundred rupees and a bag of salt. Unfortunately, we took a different route out instead of going through Sumprabum, so I didn't see you there. I'm glad I caught up with you here."

The news flattered me. Not the five hundred rupees, a small enough sum as wartime bribes went, but the bag of salt, which was really valuable. The Burmese villagers used salt in so many ways, especially for keeping fish and meat from spoiling. Cut off from normal supplies by the Japanese occupation, they had to forage at the salt licks used by animals or else barter with the enemy. What I liked best, was that the villagers never took the offer. They did without the salt, and I remained at large in the jungle.

This all began just after I had trekked out of Burma and reached Calcutta. One day I was talking with my brother-in-law and his family when somebody came along the court shouting, "Does J. Girsham live here?" I turned around and saw a young military officer. "Yes, I'm J. Girsham."

Speaking in clipped army tones, he put a half-question, half-order to me. "Will you please come down here?" Then I began to wonder if I was about to be arrested, and if so, why. One thing, I had been grumbling like everyone else about the retreat from Burma. The Burmese, the Gurkhas, and even quite a few British soldiers complained that the British command wouldn't stand and fight. I thought I might have said something the military wanted me to explain.

The officer took me in his truck to Fort William, where a colonel and a brigadier were waiting in an office. The colonel handed me a telegram. I read the following:

FIND J. GIRSHAM, 114 RIPPON STREET, CALCUTTA. INSTRUCT HIM, PROCEED DINJAN FOR SERVICE WITH THE BURMA LEVIES.

STEVENSON, COL.

"You will be commissioned a second lieutenant if you accept," the colonel said. "Do you accept?" Much relieved, I replied that I did, and when he asked when I could leave for Dinjan, I said, "Now."

Dinjan was an airfield in Assam. When I got there, I was assigned to duty with the RAF, studying the most secret reports of conditions in Burma. I spent a month on this type of intelligence work, gathering information about the Burmese who remained loyal, those who were acting as agents for the Japanese, and so on. But I was just marking time. My real assignment took me back into the Burmese jungle.

I flew from Dinjan to Fort Hertz with Colonel F. W. M. Gamble, Edmund Leech, an anthropologist who was a captain in the Burma Rifles, and a young fellow named Dennis Rosener. We started at once to form the guerrilla force called the Northern Kachin Levies.

I went to a village called Naungkhai, about thirteen miles north of Fort Hertz on the Malika River—which is really the upper part of the Irrawaddy—established myself in a little bungalow, and started recruiting jungle fighters among

133

the Kachins. These rugged mountain people joined readily, out of hatred of the Japanese, or love of battle, or to draw their military pay. I taught them to handle rifles and automatic weapons, Bren guns, and tommy guns.

The most elaborate speech I ever made went something like this: "Here's what you will do in this war. You will hunt the Japanese the way you hunt animals. We're not going to have parades and all that. We're not going to fight from prepared positions; we're going to use hit-and-run tactics. You will shoot the enemy, and you will capture him if you can, and you will get information about him in every form to hand over to the people in the rear who are organizing to come back into Burma. They'll have to know what to expect, and what they'll find, and who they'll fight, and who will be with them."

The Colonel took some of these Kachin Levies to Sumprabum, a little more than halfway to Myitkyina, which was then occupied by the Japanese. He ordered me to form a company and bring them up. I did. He then gave me fifty-four men, saying, "Here is your company. I'll complete it when we get more men in. Anyway, you go down to Myitkyina, or as far as you can in that direction."

"A fine affair," I protested jokingly. "About three thousand Japanese and fifty-four of us?"

Actually my men and I were quite happy about our orders. The Kachins were adepts at the tactics of hit-and-run warfare, which they had practiced long before the British came to Burma. And they knew their native jungles. So they felt in their element as we pushed through until we got within forty miles of Myitkyina. All the while I was talking to any local people we met, and sending runners back with any information that seemed important. I assured the villagers, "Coming up behind us from Fort Hertz there are three thousand British with mules and artillery and planes, and supplies of all sorts." I wanted this word to spread along the rivers and the roads to keep the Kachins from going over to the Japanese—and to worry the Japanese themselves.

Of course, they knew from their own intelligence work that we were in the area, and they began to consolidate their positions accordingly, pulling back outposts that seemed too exposed. We heard that sixty of the enemy were holed up in Kawapang, but they packed up and retreated as we advanced. My Kachin boys were always ready for a fight. They'd urge me, "Let's go on after them and shoot them." That wasn't part of the plan, so I'd have to reply, "No, let them go, but we'll shadow them and see what they do."

I was playing a kind of chess game with the Japanese commander opposing me, and my purpose was to find out how far his superiors would allow him to retreat. I had a very good senior man named Shing-gyi, a Kachin court interpreter in peacetime in Myitkyina, capital of the Kachin State. He and I went ahead on the trail of the Japanese, leaving the main company behind under a warrant officer who was to bring them up three or four days later.

Shing-gyi and I followed the enemy. At night we'd catch up, view their little fires on the side of the hill, and get into the grass and sleep. When we woke in the morning, we'd see them pull out again. Now I was the one itching to pull the trigger, especially at night when our quarry were silhouetted beautifully against the firelight. I used to say, "I can put a bullet in that Jap's back . . ." Shing-gyi, more prudent, would control me by pointing out that our mission was to pick up intelligence data, not get into a scrap with the enemy—not just yet, anyway.

We trailed them for forty miles. They crossed a number of minor tributaries of the Irrawaddy until they reached the Hpong-in-Kha River, where they dug in on the far bank. They evidently felt safe there because they were in direct contact with their forces in Myitkyina, twenty-six miles away, and had the advantage of good roads for motor traffic. When my company came up we dug in on the bank of the N' Sop River, with a no man's land of four miles between us. The road passed below our position, went across the N' Sop River (only about thirty yards wide), and ran straight opposite us for four to five hundred yards before it bent and led toward the Japanese on the Hpong-in-Kha.

It wasn't long before each force knew pretty well where the other was. I had to anticipate that enemy reinforcements would come up from Myitkyina, in which case there would be a battle. My left flank seemed safe because it was anchored on the river, but on the right there was only dense jungle, so I deployed most of my fifty-four men along the right flank. I kept seventeen in position with me along the road—the key point, because Colonel Gamble had told me, "You are responsible for the main road. You must hold it, once you get into position there."

After we were dug in, I ordered the river bank to be cleared to get an unimpeded firing line in case the enemy should attack from that direction. We used an old method in defending the jungle, one common among Burmese hunters. The Kachins suggested it to me, and I agreed because I had used it for hunting wild boar. We got big bamboos, sharpened the ends into spikes, and hardened them over the fire. These spears, long enough to impale a man, are called *pangees*. They are terrible weapons, their points unbreakable and sharp as a razor. In hunting, the Burmans would plant a row of *pangees* at one exit from a patch of jungle, stampede the pigs into the opening, and collect the beasts when they impaled themselves in their mad dash to get away.

Starting on the opposite bank from where we were, my men cleared the jungle on the right side of the road for an

136

area perhaps three hundred yards by fifty to a hundred yards. The trees there were small and sparse and grew amid short grass that offered no cover. My plan was to open up a good field of fire if the Japanese ran across this space for the cover higher up the slope. The other side of the road sloped downward through long grass to the river three hundred yards away. In this long grass I had the *pangees* fixed into place. The rounded butts were hammered into the earth about three feet. The hafts, three feet long, stood out at various angles to the ground, pointing toward the road. We planted many rows, the points of each row fitting into the spaces of the row ahead, alternately high and low, which gave us virtually a solid wall of deadly weapons hidden in the grass. We had fifteen thousand *pangees*—many more than we could have produced by ourselves, but some villagers came out to help us.

With the trap baited, all we required was a quarry to drive into it. When the Japanese came out in the open, and we fired at them, they naturally would dive for cover—and onto the *pangees*. That was the strategy, and one of my men, Jemadar Nawng Seng, kept reminding the rest that the enemy soldiers were near and might be advancing on us at any moment. One day, while writing notes in a trench, I heard firing in the direction of the jungle. The group assigned to clear the jungle was coming back. "What happened?"

One of them answered, "This Jemadar Nawng Seng has been putting us on guard by pretending the Japanese were attacking. Today he said the same thing, and we didn't believe him, and then we heard voices shouting, 'Hey! Hey!' And when we turned and looked, we saw two Japs gesturing at us. We put down our knives, grabbed our rifles, and fired at them. They fired back, but nobody was hit, and they ran off."

Since the Japanese had seen us, we expected them to attack. And four days later they did: Sixty or more came along the road. I had an expert Bren gunner named Zaura who wanted to open up on them at four hundred yards. "Wait," I said. "What have we got those *pangees* for? Let's not run them down the road. We want them to head into the grass when they realize we're strong enough to stop them on the road."

The Japanese moved forward without realizing they were parallel to the *pangees*. I waited until those in front reached the *pangees* nearest to our position, and then I ordered my men to open up with everything we had. We fired rifles, tommy guns, Bren guns, and all the other weapons we were armed with. We shouted and yelled abuse at the enemy. As I expected, the Japanese ran into the nearest cover, the long grass, from which there came screams and curses as they plunged into the *pangees*. I called out, "Fire wherever the grass is waving! We'll hit more of them!" And we did.

When the Japanese commander realized what was happening, he ordered his men to retreat, taking the dead and wounded with them. Later some of our agents who went into the Japanese camp to exchange fish for salt reported, "There was any number of bodies laid out in the camp. The Japanese took them away and covered them with large tarpaulins. Then they loaded them on trucks and took them back by night to headquarters in Myitkyina."

Eventually they avoided the stretch where the *pangees* lay hidden and attacked us from other angles. We pushed them back no fewer than five times. However, they had plenty of men to keep up the attacks. They would get in between the *pangees* and the river and move through the jungle to the assault, but we never let them cross the N' Sop until they brought up artillery. Since we had nothing to hit back with, we retreated, stopping at N' Gip Kha, four miles to the rear. We had a respite of only twenty-four hours, for the Japanese were on our heels with their artillery, and we had to retreat another four miles, to Tiang Zup, where we dug in and held fast. They were getting too far from their base, and they probably thought they had taught us enough of a lesson to prevent us from coming back.

One evening while we were at Tiang Zup, Colonel Gamble arrived for an on-the-spot inspection of the situation. He wasn't at all pleased with the retreat, and showed his feelings quite plainly. This was the first time he had come into the battle zone where real fighting was going on, and he might not have come just then except that he had been accepting congratulations for our previous successes. We had been sending back the spoils of war, including items of equipment taken from one dead Japanese—helmet, bayonet, grenades, rations, and parts of his uniform. These made nice exhibits for Colonel Gamble to show at headquarters. He wasn't quite so happy when we had to pull back. He demanded to know exactly what had happened at the battle of N' Sop Zup.

I didn't like having to explain, and he didn't like my explanation, so afterward I said, "Colonel, I'd like to take out a patrol and go back and see what the Japanese are doing in my old position." He agreed, so I struck into the jungle with Captain Rae, Lieutenant Butler, and Jemadar Nawng Seng.

Everything was quiet as we moved forward. Still, they could be setting a trap for us, a possibilty I began discussing with my Burmese assistant. Suddenly I figured we were too far out in the open road, in an ideal spot to be caught by an ambush. "Let's get down into the grass and the undergrowth," I suggested.

I took the lead, walking rapidly because the light was failing, and we had eight miles to go to get back to camp to report to Colonel Gamble. Abruptly I stopped moving. Something was holding my leg back. I pushed harder. My leg still wouldn't move. I looked down and saw two small *pangees* sticking right through my trousers, into my leg. Hundreds of other *pangees* looked at me hungrily from the grass, waiting for my damn fool body to fall on them.

Captain Rae was so close behind he nearly fell over me. "I'm stuck!" I exclaimed. He replied, "I'm stuck too!" Jemadar Nawng Seng, a small chap, had impaled himself through the thigh. Butler was the only one who managed to keep off those terrifying *pangees*. With his help, the rest of us got free, but we carried painful injuries back to camp.

When we reached Tiang Zup, two American officers were there, Colonel Eifler and Colonel Coughlin. They had come to see what methods I was using for jungle warfare. Seeing our wounds, they offered to take us back to Sumprabum for medical treatment, an offer we were only too happy to accept. At Sumprabum I reported to a colonel, who sent me back to base camp in Calcutta to get my leg tended.

There, after a few days at Fort Hertz, I had some drinks with an old friend, who was not impressed with my "wounded" legs. He invited me to join in a game of football. I protested feebly. He looked at the *pangee* cuts with a critical eye. "Just a flesh wound!" he pronounced. "Nothing to stop a Girsham!" Well, I agreed, and during the game I fractured my knee. Now I was laid up for five months.

They sent me to St. Luke's Hospital in Chabua. From there I went to Shillong to recuperate—and to hear about the price on my head, five hundred rupees and a bag of salt.

11

Campaigning with Merrill's Marauders

While I was laid up in St. Luke's Hospital, Eifler and Coughlin came to visit me. They said they were impressed with my knowledge of the jungle and wanted me to sign up with Merrill's Marauders when I got back on my feet. They arranged for my transfer; and after Shillong I was posted to the Ledo area for duty with the United States combat forces. I went directly to Shinbwiyang, where I had my first interview with General Merrill himself. He and his men marched from Ledo. I flew down in a light plane for the rendezvous.

Merrill and I hit it off from the start, and during the

weeks that followed I got to know him quite well. Out in the jungle we'd usually meet when he wanted an opinion about a certain place or people or route familiar to me. There were occasions when, during a break on the march, he'd say, "Jack, come and have lunch with me. Bring your own rations!" We'd sit by the side of the trail and have a relaxed discussion of whatever happened to be on his mind. He asked me to describe my childhood, my family, and my work with the Bombay Burmah Trading Corporation. He was particularly interested in my stories of elephant and tiger hunting and had hoped to come back to Burma and hunt these animals with me.

Two things impressed me about Merrill: First, he was a cool, clever, and tough fighting man, the type who would never lose his temper or his nerve. Second, as I came to learn, he cared for his men.

Of course, he had good people around him—the finest officers you could want, in my opinion. Colonel C. N. Hunter, the second in command, was much like Merrill, but with more of a temper, and not at all hesitant about stating his opinion when the higher-ups blundered. In his book, *Galahad,* he even took on "Vinegar Joe" Stilwell, the commanding general. Colonels William Osborne and George MacGee were great field commanders, willing and anxious to get up where the shooting was going on, which made the GIs respect them more than anything else. And there were others of the same caliber. Still, Merrill was running the show, and neither he nor his officers ever forgot it. I got to know most of them during the campaign, and I never noticed a hint of jealousy. Everyone was committed to doing his job.

For those who fought with Merrill most of the campaigning was behind the Japanese lines, filtering in, marching under cover, fighting. We'd cut them off whenever we could, and set traps for them, and chew up their supplies. Some battles were pretty big shows—for instance Walawbum, a solid three-day affair. Only a little stream divided us from the enemy, and we could hear practically everything they said above a whisper. That was where the Nisei boys proved so useful. One of them, Henry Gosho, translated a conversation between a Japanese officer and his men: "Who are you fighting?" the officer asked. "We don't know the units," a soldier replied, "but we do know they're Americans, and they're armed with automatic weapons." It was nice to learn they had some respect for us.

Since many of the Japanese knew English, there was much shouting across the stream in the darkness. One fellow over there would shout, "Roosevelt eats K rations!" And we'd reply, "Tojo eats ——!" Then they'd open up with their guns, wasting any amount of ammunition firing over our trenches. Here we were trying to kill each other, saving our bullets for the right moment, and suddenly we said a few vulgar words and they got too angry to hold their fire.

By the third day we were running short of ammunition. Captain Richards came along to the edge of the trenches and assigned me to help him collect ammunition and carry it to the men on the outer perimeter. By now I felt the Japanese had had their chance to pick me off and told myself, You're not going to be hit. Providence is watching over you. That's how I felt, and somehow I moved about safely, collecting and carrying ammunition.

Our men on the perimeter were able to keep shooting for a while longer, but eventually the ammunition ran out, and we couldn't depend on supplies from the rear. Besides, the Japanese had artillery, and we had only mortars. We couldn't stay where we were.

A time was set, and the whole battalion, one thousand men, started the retreat from the positions we held. The move back wasn't as silent as we'd have liked it to be. Our mules were a special problem moving through the jungle. Every time a sound disturbed them they'd bray at the top of their lungs. We had to cut their vocal cords to silence them. On top of all this, we had to move through bright moonlight.

Amazingly, we weren't attacked during the pull-out. We got away without being molested. A little later we captured a Japanese soldier, explained to him how we had retreated untouched, and asked him what had happened, why his side had left us alone all through the night. He looked at us and replied, "We pulled out an hour earlier." So we all laughed, even though we were ready to kick ourselves for not holding on a mite longer. The important thing, nevertheless, was that the Japs retreated from Walawbum. The Chinese units fighting on the Maingkhwan side were called in to occupy the abandoned village. After a couple of days' rest, we went on to a place called Nhpum Ga to reconnoiter the Japanese artillery.

General Merrill came to me one evening and announced, "Jack, at eight o'clock in the morning a plane will fly over and drop two rifles. I'm presenting one to the old chief, Zing Htoong Naw, and one to you. It's a sniper's rifle with a telescopic sight." The General was determined to turn a hunter into a soldier. It was a beautiful dual-purpose weapon.

Colonel MacGee's battalion arrived a little later, and my battalion went down the hill to make room for them. There wasn't much space for all of us. We were hemmed in when the Japanese came up, surrounded the hill, and started bombarding us. Again we were so close we could nearly touch the enemy. A water hole in between belonged to us in the morning, to the enemy at midday, and in the evening we took over again. It took some doing for us to hold out.

The mules went there to drink, and got killed by artillery shells. The stench hanging over the area was awful.

Still, we did hold out until two seventy-five-millimeter artillery pieces were dropped to us. Then we were able to hit the Japanese harder. We drove them off, and pushed on. We reached Naubum, where we found the famous Father James Stuart, the Irish missionary who helped the Marauders so much. He was a legendary figure in my Burma. Everyone knew of St. Columbine's mission in Myitkyina, where Father Stuart cared for the Kachin people during the Japanese occupation.

I was rather sick by then, not being used to a diet of K rations. I wanted something more substantial, and so did the four Kachin scouts with me. Merrill saw me in a very bad state, weak and vomiting. "Jack," he said, "ride my horse. We'll get you to Naubum and see what can be done for you. What's wrong, anyway?" I answered, "My men and I are not used to K rations." So the General sent a signal for an air drop of food at Naubum.

One day, as we moved forward, I saw a European wearing a scout hat coming toward me on the trail. He greeted me: "Hello, Jack!" At first I hadn't the faintest idea who he was, but when he uncovered, to my joy, I recognized Father Stuart. I had the pleasure of introducing him to General Merrill, who was coming up behind.

We all marched on to Naubum. There Father Stuart provided us with Indian rations, inviting my scouts to have their share. We had never seen anything like it. We collected our meat, and our curry, and one whole eighty-pound bag of rice apiece.

Food is all-important in the jungle. The American soldiers didn't understand it at first. They watched the Kachin scouts and me picking mushrooms or tender bamboo shoots and catching the fish we poisoned in the streams with roots

145

and bark, and remained puzzled until they tried our diet. Then the Americans would eat rice and the stuff we ate whenever they could. They agreed with us that K rations were too light for the rigors of jungle warfare.

After the short stay at Naubum, we went on toward Myitkyina. Colonel Hunter was especially anxious to keep moving on to that town, but the higher-ups wouldn't let him. They overestimated the Japanese strength confronting us. And so Myitkyina wasn't recaptured for another three months. The campaign cost us good men, many of them young chaps fresh from America. At the end we had only about 400 of the original Merrill's Marauders. The newcomers joining us fought well despite their losses, and after some hard campaigning against strengthened Japanese units, we finally took Myitkyina.

Just about here, General Merrill went back to the hospital, suffering from heart trouble. We heard he had continued on to Ceylon and become an aide to Lord Louis Mountbatten, who was planning the over-all strategy for war in the Far East. Merrill never came back for our hunt.

The Marauders didn't last much longer than their commanding general. Colonels Hunter and MacGee received new orders and left. Their soldiers were placed in a grouping called the Mars Force. I was among those who stayed, and we set out to cut the Burma Road. We went through sparsely inhabited areas with few villages, climbing mountains where the vegetation differed from the rain forest we were used to. We passed from low cane brakes, bamboo thickets, swamps, and that sort of terrain in the Hukong Valley to country where tall trees overlooked green grass. Here it was easy going in cold, dry weather—nothing like the Hukong Valley, where when you lay down to take your ten-minute break you had leeches all over you.

We got to the Burma Road north of Lashio before we had

any contact with the Japanese. We made Nawkhum village our base of operations, complete with artillery, although all we were really doing was mopping up the Japanese who tried to break through back to Siam. They weren't looking for a fight when they came down the Burma Road by night—they wanted to get away because they knew they had been beaten in Burma. We could see their car headlights, so we'd go with bazookas, set up an ambush by the side of the road, and shoot up their convoys.

Before this operation ended, we were stationed on a ridge of hills about a mile from the opposite ridge, where Japanese soldiers were stationed. Here, one day, I joined an American friend, Ken Stager, an ornithologist from Los Angeles, who was in charge of heavy weapons on the high grounds. We went up where we could look across to the Japanese on the opposite ridge. Ken fired on them. They disappeared pretty quickly, but when the firing stopped, they came back.

I pointed to one and remarked, "I bet I can hit that fellow with my new rifle." Ken thought we were too far for an accurate shot. I did miss, but the bullet must have come close because my target at least ducked! We could afford to play games by now. The war was just about over.

When we attacked the position, we drove the Japanese off in less than two hours. And it was here that World War II ended for us. We had cut the Burma Road. The Japanese couldn't use it any more for their convoys, and those who escaped after tremendous losses had to slip back through the jungle into Siam. We saw the Burma Road littered with the equipment we had shot up and smashed—their tanks, trucks, command cars, artillery pieces, every kind of military hardware imaginable.

We were wondering what would happen to us next, when Colonel Mackie came along looking for Ken Stager. The Colonel was doing some research on typhus, which so many

Chinese suffered from. He wanted an ornithologist to come
to his camp at Myitkyina to identify the birds and animals
that carried the germs, and to perform laboratory tests that
might reveal the nature of the disease and lead to a cure.

Ken was willing. He pointed out to Colonel Mackie that
much hunting and trapping would be involved. "You'll need
a jungle man too," he said, "somebody who knows the
wildlife of Upper Burma. We've got the best candidate for
the job right here: name, Jack Girsham." The reassignment
took time because they had to make arrangements for me
to leave my unit officially and join the American Typhus
Commission.

Once there, my job was in the field, setting up snares and
traps for wild rats, jungle cats, gerbils, monkeys, jungle
fowl, and so on. I brought these creatures in, and I gathered
bugs, ticks, and lice from their ears and the surrounding
areas of fur or feathers. I even collected plants and grass
that had been in contact with typhus victims. All this evidence underwent a scientific inspection in our lab, a building equipped with the best medical facilities the American
officers in charge could assemble.

The technical science was new to me. Once I shot a jungle
fowl and noticed five or six small ticks, each about the size
of a pinhead, in its feathers next to the ears. At the lab an
assistant called me to the microscope: there were hundreds
of tiny creatures much too small to be seen by the naked
eye. Of course, I had never been aware of such microscopic
life in the jungle. I had read of such things, but this work
opened up a whole new view of nature for me.

Ken Stager used to say he thought he and I made good
partners for typhus research. As a trained ornithologist, he
could tell me things I never knew about natural history. As
a jungle man, I could give him lessons about the behavior
of birds and animals in their natural habitat. I had never seen

microscopic germs before. He had never heard a tiger bell like a sambar, or a king cobra imitate the call of a jungle fowl. So we had much to tell each other. It was a good partnership.

12

Back to
the Jungle

I liked my work with the Typhus Commission, especially because it took me back to the jungle, as adviser to an enthusiastic amateur.

Colonel Mackie was fascinated by the big cats. One evening he drove off to another military unit for dinner, and the following day he was very excited. "Jack," he said, "just outside our camp as I drove up I saw a tiger as big as an ox. He was so close I thought he was going to walk into my jeep. In fact, he nearly collided with my bumper. There must be plenty of tigers around here. Do you think I could bag one?"

GIRSHAM: Sure, why not?

MACKIE: What kind of weapon will I shoot it with?

GIRSHAM: A shotgun.

MACKIE: A shotgun? Impossible!

He really thought I was joking and kept protesting that there wasn't enough hitting power in a shotgun to bring down a tiger. I insisted that it was the proper weapon and finally persuaded him to give the shotgun a try.

Shortly after that conversation a tiger made a kill not far from our camp. I told Mackie that the tiger would probably return and might give him a good shot if he wanted to sit up. He liked the idea, so I had a machan built over the remains of the dead animal. I had to go somewhere else that night, but I left him with buckshot cartridges with twelve pellets in each. I told him to stay on the machan until eleven o'clock at the latest, and that if the cat didn't come by then it wouldn't come at all that night.

I got an experienced boy to sit up with him. "This boy has a flashlight," I said to the Colonel. "When you hear the tiger at the kill, the boy will flash his light on the place where the sound is coming from. You'll be able to see clearly enough to get in a good shot. If you aim behind the shoulder, one shot may do the trick." Then I left the two on the machan.

The next day I met Colonel Mackie. He told me how he and the boy had waited patiently until about ten o'clock, when they heard a tiger approaching. The big cat moved up to the kill, crouched down, and began to have another meal. At that moment, the boy turned on his flashlight. The Colonel needed only one shot to bag his quarry. He confessed, "Jack, I didn't believe you when you said a shotgun could bring down a tiger. Last night you made a believer of me." He had learned what I had known since I was a boy: that the tiger has a thin skin and comparatively light fur, easily penetrated by buckshot—unlike the elephant or the boar or the buffalo, creatures with tough hides that require a high-powered rifle.

Back to the Jungle

My tour of duty with the Typhus Commission lasted until 1945. I remained in the Burmese army for another four years, mostly in Maymyo, where my old home-town acquaintances were startled to see me after so many years. They hadn't heard about my fighting the Japanese, and didn't know whether I was dead or alive. The local people invited me to come back to their areas for some hunting, the type of invitation I liked best. The officers from headquarters often accompanied me; the commander, Colonel Cook, was especially fond of shooting jungle fowl.

But things began to change. While the older Burmans remained friendly, the younger ones became unfriendly. Independence from British colonial rule brought a whole new set of politicians into power, and although I personally had no interest in politics, I could see the results of the "Burma for the Burmans" campaign. Nationalists were in the saddle, and one thing they had taken over from the colonial regime was a superior attitude toward those who weren't "our kind." The new pukka sahibs were Burmans with relatives in the Rangoon government; they got the cushy jobs and high salaries, and the tough, dangerous assignments were handed to the Anglo-Burmans. This attitude made it more and more difficult for me to get along with them, and in the end I gave up trying and resigned my commission and left Burma for good.

I wanted to remain in hunting and game control, so I applied for a warden's job in Tanganyika—and I got it. Of course I didn't know Africa. But I did know big game, and the people there thought if I could keep tigers and bison in order, I ought to be able to handle lions and rhinos as well. I thought so too.

At the time I was engaged to my second wife, Charmaine, who lived in Calcutta. I went to Assam to pay my respects to the doctors and nurses who had treated my war injuries at St. Luke's Hospital. I received a letter from Charmaine's brother: "On your way back to Calcutta, touch in at Shillong and see the senior official in charge of forests. He wants to speak to you."

I went to Shillong to see this man. He said, "I hear you're going to Tanganyika to take a job." I nodded. He frowned and toyed with a pencil. "Why do you want to go all the way to Africa when there's a job waiting for you right here in Assam? I need a Game Warden. The position is open right now, it's yours for the taking, and I'd like you to take it. Will you?"

This was one decision that didn't take any time or thought. If I had been allowed to select my own opportunity, I would have mentioned Game Warden of Assam, which, of course, is next to Burma and quite like it.

"I'll take it," I told the official. "In fact, it solves my personal problem. My only reason for going to Africa was to stay in the hunting business. I'd much rather remain in an area I'm familiar with. Besides, I'd rather deal with tigers than any other wild animals."

He looked as gratified as I was. "Fine!" he said. "I'll put the application through to the central government in Delhi. In the meantime, while we're waiting for approval to come through, here's a license. You're qualified to shoot elephants doing damage to crops and rogue elephants, when calls come in from the local authorities. Also dangerous animals, like man-eaters, will be your responsibility."

Delighted with my good luck, I took the license, went into the jungle, and started shooting elephants that were ravaging paddy fields and tearing up tea gardens. My employers were local officials and tea planters, both of whom, frequently, were willing to pay me to get rid of the same dangerous animal or bothersome herd. I often worked for tea estates on a season's contract, taking care of their problems from October to March.

To get to know Assam and its people, I went to village hunting festivals whenever I could. I enjoyed watching the villagers during their three-day celebrations. They'd grab their spears, bows, and knives, and beat through the jungle, flushing animals and trying to run down those suitable for the pot. There was constant shouting and scrambling, cries of triumph when the game was caught, and satirical laughter when it escaped an inept hunter. Back at the village, they'd cook the meat and hold a banquet. Next morning, some men would be "ready" for the hunt who hadn't slept all night because they'd been feasting and carousing.

I went hunting on my own, ran safaris for people who had come to Assam to shoot big game—and I took on odd assignments. That's how I happened to get involved with Lowell Thomas and his crew on the television tiger hunt.

The years in Assamese game control were good ones for me, although I never became Game Warden of Assam. I renewed my license from year to year, so I was able to keep on earning my living out in the jungle with my gun. Charmaine and I were married and lived in Calcutta, a two-hour flight to Assam. Off duty, I'd fly south and spend my time with her in the city on the Hooghly, where we had a lot of relatives and friends and she had a job.

Looking back, I suppose the rejection of my application for Game Warden was the handwriting on the wall. Even more than Burma—indeed influencing Burma in this respect —India was nationalistic. As the years passed, antiforeign feeling grew stronger among those who now held power, and among the rank and file who followed them. It was only natural that non-Indian officials and officers were phased out, replaced by Indians.

So Charmaine and I decided to leave India. Basically, we chose between two places. My sister was living in New Zealand, which was my preference. However, Charmaine's relatives were mainly in England, and she wanted to be with them. Since I wanted her to be where she would be happiest, we decided on England.

While we were planning, I told nobody beyond our immediate circle. I never resigned from the hunting job in Assam, but just quietly let my license lapse by not requesting a renewal. A friend promised me, "I'm going to send in your license every year and have it renewed while you're away. Then you'll have it ready if you come back to India." I let him take the document and said I appreciated the gesture; but we both realized I'd never hunt in Assam again.

The hunting license lapsed in March 1967. In August Charmaine and I left Calcutta for London.

We settled in New Barnet, just outside London. As Anglo-Burmans, we had always considered Britain "home," but at times I'm oddly homesick. For while the countryside has the charm we used to read about, I love the jungle, which, though it can be a place of terror and is nearly always uncomfortable, remains my spiritual home. A thousand personal memories are at my beck and call, from the safaris I've run to the "feel" of the breeze heralding the oncoming monsoon. I can recall Pegu, Maymyo and Shillong—and many a nameless village—as good places to be. I know what it's like to play with a baby elephant, to sit on a machan waiting for a tiger, to draw a bead on a sambar, to scout the teak forest in the early morning when the jungle fowl are beginning to rustle and the cry of the barking deer echoes through the hills. I wish I could go back. But if I can't, at least I've been there.